THE NINE HALLS OF DEATH

THE NINE HALLS OF DEATH

OF DEATH

✦ ✦ ✦ ✦ ✦ ✦ ✦ ✦

NINJA SECRETS OF
MIND MASTERY

DR. HAHA LUNG

CITADEL PRESS
Kensington Publishing Corp.
www.kensingtonbooks.com

CITADEL PRESS BOOKS are published by

Kensington Publishing Corp.
850 Third Avenue
New York, NY 10022

All Kensington titles, imprints, and distributed lines are available at special quantity discounts for bulk purchases for sales promotions, premiums, fund-raising, educational, or institutional use. Special book excerpts or customized printings can also be created to fit specific needs. For details, write or phone the office of the Kensington special sales manager: Kensington Publishing Corp., 850 Third Avenue, New York, NY 10022, attn: Special Sales Department; phone 1-800-221-2647.

CITADEL PRESS and the Citadel logo are Reg. U.S. Pat. & TM Off.

First printing: February 2007

10 9 8 7 6 5 4 3 2 1

Printed in the United States of America

Library of Congress Control Number: 2006934742

ISBN-13: 978-0-8065-2801-4

ISBN-10: 0-8065-2801-X

To

Marian S. Tucker,

Mother and Muse

and to

Christopher B. Prowant, Eddie Harris,

and the warriors of the Zendokan.

MASAKATSU!

CONTENTS

CONTENTS

CONTENTS

INTRODUCTION: "Darkness seeks what Darkness needs . . ."

SOMEWHERE FAR ACROSS THAT TURBULENT SEA FLOATS AN island kingdom as dark and mysterious by night as it is brilliantly lit by day.

Yet, too much light blinds as surely as too little.

At the heart of this xenophobic realm grows an impenetrable black forest, ages old, equally shadowed by day as it is when embraced by Mother Night.

Many are the paths leading into this foreboding forest, yet only one path leads out from this dark wood: success.

Ignoring that wizened philosopher who warned us against staring overlong into the Abyss, down through the ages many have stood staring overlong at this seeming "shortcut" to wealth, glory, and power, and perhaps even enlightenment. And yet, faced with the prospect of finally placing that first foot forward onto the path, so many pull up short, instead humbling their heads as they settle for a more roundabout—safer!—road to realizing their dreams.

For while the path is open to all, of those who do undertake the journey, few will finish. Yet, all who dare—who survive!—grow stronger of wit and will for having merely dared that first step. For the path itself—rough and rock-strewn for many, surprisingly smooth for others—is but the first step in an important—unforgiving!—primal selection process; separating the wheat from the chaff, the pearl from the oyster, the quick from the dead.

The journey of a thousand *minds* begins with a single step.

And what do those hardy few who fearlessly tread the path find patiently awaiting them at the heart of that great forest?

A sudden clearing! Where, to our surprise, we discover not just our own path terminating, but many other paths heretofore unsuspected, all converging, or, if we reverse our perspective, a *mandala*-like sun source of power radiating outward, dedicated to holding back that most dangerous of darkness: the darkness of ignorance.

At the center of this unexpected clearing sits a weathered lodge, expertly hidden by bramble and briar, overtaken by vine and vintage.

A monastery? A prison? A temple. Or a house of temptation?

Not all see with equal eye.

Whether refuge or rack and ruin, this lodge's forbidding archway, engraved with all manner of warning cut in languages long dead, guarded by the deeply carved demons and dragons etched there, dares us to draw deeper within, beckoning us—not to warmth, comfort, and rest—but to discomfort and chaos, the true handmaidens of Change.

No sooner do we step first foot over that threshold, than we realize the illusionary smallness and simplicity of the lodge's exterior was but a mask for a vast—perhaps endless!—interior, one that both defies physical proportion and challenges mental preconception.

Beyond this portal, an extended passage, one haunted by a hint of menace, guarded by purposeful myth and perhaps the last vestige of true magic!

Finally, we find the nine doors branching off from this corridor, each one of which leads into one of Nine Halls . . .

. . . *The* Nine Halls, those semimythical chambers of training and testing wherein are kept the collective knowledge of masters past.

It is these Nine Halls that vouchsafe the adroit skills and arcane scrolls that lead to power, and to powers only whispered about in myth, or shouted out during bouts of terminal madness!

Herein dwells the masterful—near mystical!—mix of myth and

magic, truth and falsehood; where physical mastery melds with mental acuity to become a third thing, something . . . more . . .

But dare we say more?

Those who speak do not know.

Those who know dare not speak.

But those who dare the Nine Halls *will* know all.

And, knowing all . . . what further will we then fear to dare!

•

THE NINE HALLS OF DEATH

I. HISTORY

⚡

INTRODUCTION: *"MYTH, MADNESS, AND MAYHEM"*

WHO AND WHAT WERE "THE NINJA"? WE'VE READ the books, we've seen the movies, we've even played the video games. But who were these mysterious warriors? Did they live up to their deadly reputations or is all that just good (or bad?) PR?

Today, Ninja are portrayed in books and movies as "superwarriors," mysterious and blackmasked, armed to the teeth with an impossible arsenal of arcane weapons; unstoppable master killers, single-handedly performing fantastic feats of daring-do designed to maim, murder, and spread mayhem!

Unlike so many other "bait-and-switch" offers, the Ninja *do* live up to much of their hype. Their's was a violent time that demanded equally violent responses.

Were the Ninja warriors of old really magicians who could walk through walls, walk on water, and walk away with a victim's head no matter how well guarded he was?

The quick answer to that is "Yes!" But to truly understand—and *master!*—the Ninja realm, we must steel our souls to venturing deeper into the dark, seemingly impenetrable realm ruled by these fiercest and most feared of warriors—and once there, to spirit away the lost key to their craft—to make that craft our own!

First, however, we must answer the question: what is a Ninja? Part mayhem, part madness and murder—all mystery! And to answer this and other "forbidden" questions, we must be willing to both sacrifice and "shapeshift": to sacrifice our petty daily delights and distractions, to transform "leisure time" into study time.

"Ninja" don't have "leisure time." There will be time enough for "leisure" when you're *dead!*

But before we are so quick to don our $9.95 polyester "Authentic Ninja mask" and start stumbling around in the darkened underbrush, it might behoove us to first learn a little something about medieval Japan, for no elite cadre is created in a vacuum, neither do they operate in one. Like modern-day terrorists, all such killer cadre are products of their times and environment.

Japanese society in the Middle Ages was rigidly structured with each person knowing his place and purpose in family, clan, and state. At the top of the heap, true power lay in the heavy hands of the Samurai-warrior class. The Samurai were, in turn, at the beck and call of their supreme leader: the *Shogun*.

On paper at least, the Shogun owed his loyalty to the Emperor of Japan, a direct descendant of the gods. In truth, medieval Japanese Shoguns ruled with absolute power, enforcing their will by the swords of their Samurai.

The Samurai, in turn, were kept in check by a self-imposed code of conduct: the Bushido (lit. "The Way of the Warrior"; *bushi* means "warrior," *do* means "way, path").

Bushido mandated that a Samurai must fight foes face to face and perish with sword in hand, slain by an equal or, at worst, die by his own hand in ritualized suicide *(seppuku,* aka *hari-kiri)* designed to regain lost honor.

The code of Bushido was the ideal and not always the reality, with many Samurai falling quite short of the ideal.

While the ideal was indeed lofty, in practice each Samurai had his own idea of how the code of Bushido applied to him. Hardly surprising, Bushido was often ignored when expedient or profitable. *Victory* was the ultimate determinant whether or not the code had been crossed. Winners write the history books.

Common folk were expected to pay homage to the code of Bushido, which meant doing anything your Samurai "betters" demanded of you.

Punishment was swift and keen for any commoner daring to challenge this system in general and the wrath of Samurai in particular.

But not all kowtowed to the Samurai overlords. In the heavily forested central part of Japan lived several clans collectively known as "the *Shinobi*". We know them today as "the Ninja."*

Shinobi folk cared little for Code Bushido and they weren't the type to scare easy.

Though at first glance the Shinobi appeared to be simple farmers abiding by the mores of "civilized" Japanese society, in reality, Shinobi in general and Shinobi Ninja in particular cared little for the accepted Samurai rules of conduct, especially when it came to combat.

Fighting from a deficit position to begin with, Ninja were not about to give their Samurai foes further advantage by standing toe to toe with them.

Like modern terrorists, Ninja struck where least expected, using techniques deliberately designed to inject maximum terror into the hearts of any survivors.

Unlike a Samurai, whose loyalties might be torn between the

---

*Throughout this book, Ninja with a capital "N" is used interchangeably with "Shinobi," specifying the particular clans of "Shinobi Ninja" that existed in medieval Japan. Ninja with a small "n" is used generically to refer to anyone whose lifestyle or livelihood requires them to employ stealth and skulduggery.

Emperor, his Shogun, and his own clan and family, a Shinobi Ninja's only loyalty was to his clan. Since he could not openly carry arms (a right reserved to Samurai), Ninja seldom stood face to face with Samurai, preferring instead the safety and efficiency of striking down his enemy before that enemy even suspected an assassin was near.

The Ninja style of fighting was, and still is, "lightning and frightening guerrilla-style hit-and-run attacks."

In the same way we today find ourselves frustrated in our war against elusive terrorists who strike from the shadows with no regard for the "rules" of "civilized combat," so too the Samurai of medieval Japan found themselves powerless to thwart the Ninja.

Despite superior numbers and (what seemed to be) superior firepower, the Samurai proved powerless to prevent Ninja appearing at will, wreaking havoc, and then just as quickly disappearing.

Samurai never respected Ninja, but they did learn early on to *fear* them!

Remember that, for Samurai, striking an enemy from behind or killing him with poison was considered cowardly.

To Ninja, such *effective* tactics and techniques were only common sense. Why give an enemy a chance to strike back or defend himself, the Shinobi reasoned.

Samurai thought it very unsportsmanlike of the Ninja not to stand still long enough to be cut down.

Ninja knew death is death no matter what direction it came from!

Like their equally feared and equally despised killer cousins, the *Hashishin* "Assassins" of the Middle East (Lung, 1997B), and the *Sthaha* "Thugs" of India (Lung, 1995), terror was the main weapon in the Ninja's arsenal.

So feared and hated were the Shinobi Ninja that at one point during the 1600s mere mention of the word "ninja" merited the death penalty under the Shogun's law.

The Ninja rightly deserved their reputation of terror since they used any and all methods of murder and mayhem to bring down any foe foolish enough to challenge them, all the while instilling lasting—paralyzing!—terror in any foe *Ninja decided* to leave alive.

These methods included developing an awesome array of tactics, techniques, tools, and tricks intended to inspire awe and terror in their enemies. This doesn't mean medieval Ninja were actually the ridiculously armed "superwarriors" depicted in the movies, quite the opposite.

Truth be known, Shinobi Ninja generally operated in teams, with each warrior a specialist in one or two areas needed for a given operation. Thus, Ninja operations more closely resembled the well-planned and efficiently executed operations of today's Special Forces and Navy SEALS, where each team member's skill(s) overlap the specialties of his companions, guaranteeing the success of the operation.

On a typical mission, one Ninja, adept at perimeter penetration, would lay the groundwork for ingress into the target site: castle, compound, or camp by picking locks, scaling walls, and so on.

Once the team had gained entrance, a second ninja, an expert in unarmed combat (Jp. *Taijutsu*) would quickly and quietly remove bothersome sentries. Meanwhile, a third team member would carry out the actual intelligence-gathering or silent assassination.

Simultaneously, a fourth Ninja would be setting boobytraps designed to cover the team's primary *and secondary* avenue(s) of escape.

Myriad tales can be found of individual Ninja courage and ingenuity, but teamwork was the key to success to most Shinobi Ninja operations; with each team member called on to use to the fullest skills he had acquired while sweating his way through "The Nine Halls" of Ninjutsu.

So if the ninja were not the superwarriors we imagine them to be, why should we bother to study Ninjutsu?

No system of martial arts is perfect. Gasp!

The art doesn't make the man, the man makes the art.

Whether *Ninjutsu* is our chosen art, or whether we are just wise enough to realize that we might one day have to defend ourselves against enemies armed with "ninja" tactics, we can greatly benefit by studying the way of the Ninja.

First, by understanding the cold tactics and techniques of medieval Japanese Ninja "terrorists" and by understanding the times and circumstances that allowed them to florish, we can better evolve stratagies to combat our own present strain of terrorist virus.

Second, over the centuries the Shinobi warriors of Japan amassed an incredible body of defensive and offensive combat knowledge; knowledge that we would do well to adopt and adapt into our modern needs for self-defense.

Perhaps you feel safe and secure in your little world . . . perhaps your TV and radio have been in the repair shop since September 11, 2001?

In his *Street Ninja: Ancient Secrets for Mastering Today's Mean Streets* (1995), the author and accomplished street-fighter Dirk Skinner addresses this faulty—potentially fatal!—kind of thinking:

> The average person today might feel far removed from, and having nothing in common with, medieval Japanese Ninja. Those who take the time to study history, however, will find that the once powerful Shinobi-Ninja clans of medieval Japan started out as disenfranchised Samurai, dispossessed farmers, and persecuted followers of unpopular religious sects. Surrounded by brigands and bandits, subject to unreasonable search and seizure, forbidden to possess weapons under penalty of death, medieval Ninja survived by their cunning and by the honing of their craft. Through sweat and determination, the Shinobi clans grew stronger until brigands and bandits no longer saw them as easy prey, their clan lands ripe for the taking, their sons and daughters easy pickings. The Ninja's solidarity and willingness to resist continued to grow to where even the tyrannical despots began to fear their wrath and left them alone. Many today see no parallels,

no connection, between those Ninja of long ago and those struggling to survive in our modern world. They see no homeless, no hordes of dispossessed and disenfranchised whose angry voices grow louder every day. They see no religious persecution, no one subject to the arbitrary exercise of authority, illegal search and seizure, and the confiscation of weapons. Fortunately . . . *Street Ninja see with different eyes.*

MYTH OF THE NINJA

One of the most useful weapons in the Shinobi Ninja bag of tricks was—and still is—the superstitious awe and fear mere mention of the name "Ninja" holds for most people.

The Shinobi themselves did all they could to encourage such superstitions, especially when it came to their own mysterious comings and goings. The Shinobiman realized fear born of superstition could help him defeat an enemy just as surely as a *ninpo* (sword) or envenomed *shuriken* (throwing star).

Partially as a result of deliberate encouragement on the part of Ninja themselves, numerous myths developed over the centuries speculating on the true origin of the Ninja—most of those myths were spread by the Shinobi themselves!

Long before Black Ops terms like "propaganda" and "disinformation" came into use, the Shinobi Ninja of medieval Japan had already perfected the "Black Science" of messing with an enemy's head (see "Kyonin-no-jutsu" in the Ninth Hall).

How much of their own mythology "PR" the Ninja themselves actually believed, we may never know.

For some Ninja, especially neophytes, encouraging the belief in the Ninjas' unique mythology-cum-history gave them an added boost of confidence.

For others, those more seasoned and savvy, encouraging such superstition was merely a ploy designed to further unnerve enemies.

Gods and Goblins

The mythology of the Shinobi realm traces the origin of the Ninja back to the very creation of Japan by the brother and sister gods Izanagi and Izanami.

Izanagi thrust his sacred spear deep into the primeval waters of creation and the water dripping off his spear became the islands of Japan.

Izanagi then plucked out his eyeballs and his right eye became the sun, personified by the goddess Amaterasu. His left eye became the moon god.

The Emperors of Japan trace their lineage back to Amaterasu.

From the moon god sprang Susano, the god of storms.

Already at this early point in Ninja mythology, we see the Shinobi distancing themselves, if only symbolically, from the powers that be. For while the Imperial line traced itself back to the sun, Shinobi Ninja claimed descendance from the moon god, via Susano, the storm god.

Susano, the *"swift"* and *"impetuous"* diety, is depicted as being heavily bearded. This in itself is telling given the relative hairlessness of Japanese and adds credence to speculation that the god Susano was probably adopted and adapted by the Japanese from the *Ainu* (Jp. "Hairy ones"), the original Caucasian inhabitants of the Japanese islands.

It is Susano, according to mythology, who planted strands from his great beard, from which the great forest of Japan sprang forth.

As a result of this, Susano is the patron god of Japanese forests, and forests play an important part in the actual history of the Shinobi realm.

Traditionally, the Ninja have been associated with two types of mythical demons. The first of these demons were *Oni,* fierce, beast-like demons usually clothed in animal skins and credited with being able to shapeshift into various animal forms.

1. Oni demon

The second demon-type are the *Tengu*.

Tengu are part man, part bird—crow and other darkwings, carrion of Death, being most closely associated with them.

Tengu live in clans, each clan ruled over by a wizened *Jodan* (Lord).

Also known as *kinjin* ("goblins"), Tengu lived in trees, in those forests sacred to Susano, from whom they claim descent.

When they shapeshifted into the form of men, Tengu wore pointed black hats and covered themselves with small cloaks, often made of straw or feathers.

In their "natural" form, Tengu had long birdlike beaks and were winged (though some attributed their wings to those feathered cloaks they were known to sport).

Likewise, when they masqueraded as men, their beaks were transformed into extremely long noses.

Tengu were usually black in color, though occasionally an especially magical red Tengu would be reported.

Tengu reportedly possessed the secret of invisibility—though some believed this power actually resided in their magical cloaks. Tengu also possessed any number of other magical abilities, depending on who was telling the tale.

Japan's greatest hero, Minimoto Yoshitsune (aka Ushiwara), is said to have learned his martial arts while a refugee hiding among the Tengu.

Ushiwara's bosom companion and bodyguard, a young *Yamabushi* priest named *Benkei Oni-Waka* (translation "Devil Youth") is said to have been half-man, half-Tengu.

It is easy to see how later generations would have preferred the legend of Ushiwara learning his martial skills from mythical Tengu instead of the unpalatable truth of his studying with the despised—and feared!—Shinobi Ninja!

2. Tengu-Ninja

The mythology of the Ninja is so obvious, even a blind man could see the fact behind the fiction.

People often hide fears and fancies that don't fit within their limited little world behind a black curtain of superstition and myth.

Faced with shadow-warriors who could seemingly penetrate any guarded castle and strike down a target at will before then vanishing without a trace, it's little wonder stunned and shaken guards and superstitious servants preferred to rationalize to others (and to themselves) the sudden death of their Lord in terms of him being killed by "demons" rather than to admit to others (and to themselves) that they were powerless to stay the Ninja assassin's hand.

Truth be known, much of the miraculous abilities ascribed to Ninja were probably fabricated by witnesses who, first, because they couldn't believe what they'd seen, just made up stories.

Second, Samurai were loathe to admit their own shortcomings, to admit they'd been outsmarted by lowly Ninja.

Thus, we are left to wonder if the description of the Tengu were purposely imitated by the Ninja in an effort to further their own propaganda or whether, on the other hand, "eyewitness accounts" of Ninja lent added fuel to Tengu legends. This is obviously a case of "which came first, the chicken or the egg?"

The manner in which Ninja agents clothed themselves, the fact that the great Shinobi clans favored dense forests, and the fact they were led by Jodan-chieftains the same as the Tengu of legend, all point to the Ninja being the basis for the Tengu myth . . . and/or vice versa.

Circumstances both cultural, economic, and philosophical separated Shinobi from Samurai.

Just as those ass-kissing at the Imperial court thumbed their noses at their "backward" provincial cousins, so too Shinobi didn't think too highly of the posturing of Samurai nor the perfidious petty bickering of the Imperial court.

It's little wonder then Shinobi traced themselves mythically, if not ideologically, back to the moon god, as opposed to the Imperial lines that had descended from the sun goddess.

Still, their having "descended" from gods themselves, in this case Susano, gave the Shinobi some "bragging rights" of their own and, for some, gave them justification—if not *divine sanction*—to carry on their shadowy comings and goings outside respectable Japanese society.

Ninja . . . Who and What?

Today, when we in the West hear the word "Ninja," we automatically think of slashing Samurai blades, flashing "Ninja fighting stars" flying through the mist, and masked men—part martial artists/part magicians—leaping fifty feet into the air, walking on water and through solid walls—untouchable, mysterious masters of death and mayhem.

So what and who is a "ninja"? Who are these mysterious spy-assassins and do they still ply their trade today or was their terror and power confined to Japan's bloody feudal period?

More important still, how can we unlock their secrets?

Were ninja confined only to Japan or can "ninja" be found in other times and climes.

What is a "Ninja?" The secret is in the name itself.

Nin is an action verb meaning "to enter by stealth." In feudal Japan, this word meant sneaking in somewhere, and anyone who did so—thief, spy, or assassin—was accused of "Nin-ja."

Today, in the West, "ninja" is most often used *incorrectly* as a noun to identify a black-garbed Japanese assassin.

To further complicate matters, there is the generic use of "ninja" (small "n"), meaning anyone who employs stealth, versus the more specific "Ninja" (big "N"), referring to those clans situated primarily in the forests of Iga and Koga provinces in central Japan.

In addition, it's important we recognize that "ninja" were not—are not—just confined to Japan, since our working definition of

WESTERN "NINJA"

U.S. Navy Seals
Green Berets
Rangers
S.W.A.T.

Russian Spetsnaz

CQC martial artists

Middle Eastern terrorists
Misc. criminal cadre

HISTORICAL

Assassins (Persia/Syria)
Scarii (Israel)
Wolfshirts (Europe)

EASTERN "NINJA"

Shinobi
Yakuza
Black Dragons

Indonesian
"Nightsiders"

Indian Thuggee

Vietnamese
Black Flags

Cao Dai
Black Crows

3. "Imitation is the highest form of flattery"

"ninja" takes in anyone who uses stealth in their work. This expanded definition includes various styles of *realistic* martial arts, schools of espionage, combat and counterespionage groups, and killer cadre down through the ages.

By not limiting our definition and understanding of what exactly is a Ninja, we can open our minds to new and more diverse training methods—tricks and techniques—designed to make us even more efficient in our own craft and to help better ensure our own survival.

Under this new, expanded umbrella of "What Is Ninja?" we include:

- *Moshuh Nanren,* the ancient assassins/spies of China, from whom many of the techniques later perfected by medieval Japanese Shinobimen were derived (Lung, 1997A)
- The dreaded Kali-worshipping *Thuggee* cult of India (Lung, 1995)
- The dagger-wielding *Hashishiin* "Assassins" of the medieval Middle East (Lung, 1997B)
- Modern "Special Forces" cadres such as the U.S. Rangers, Green Beret, and Navy SEALS, as well as Soviet (now Russian) Spetsnaz and other specially trained night fighters.
- Covert operations agents
- Treacherous terrorist groups

In fact, any accomplished hitman, burglar, and other criminal whose "trade" demands skullduggery and stealth must be allowed to join our ninja (small "n") alumni list.

But that's okay, for there is much we can learn from *all* "ninja."

So, rather than cluttering or making more complicated our study of the Ninja craft, our realizing that *Ninjutsu* (the art of the Ninja) need not be confined to just medieval Japan, nor need we confine our study to mastering possibly "outdated" *traditional* Ninja martial arts techniques, our expanded definition of "What is Ninja?" opens up new and exciting areas of study.

Thus, while the answer to "What is Ninja?" might take us a lifetime to unlock, "Who is Ninja?" is more easily answered.

Who is Ninja?

You are Ninja!

NINJA RISING!

The history of the Ninja realm is shrouded in mystery. This includes the origins of the Ninja. Were it not so, Ninja would not have survived long enough to pass their deadly arts down to us.

There is safety—and power!—in secrecy. The less our enemies know about us, the better our chances of both surviving and prospering.

For the uninitiated, when it comes to anything having to do with the Shinobi realm, it is indeed difficult to sift fact from fiction.

The more difficult the quest, the brighter shines the goal and grail at the end.

As we've already established, our definition of "ninja" is a broad one, taking in a lot of territory, and includes the study of espionage cults, secret societies, and even criminal cadre—those who, by hook or by crook, either imitated or outright stole so much of their technique from the "true" Ninja of yesteryear, the *Shinobi* Ninja of medieval Japan.

But we must start somewhere, and the most obvious place would be, not with the Shinobi Ninja themselves, but further back still, to those who inspired—indeed, incited!—the Shinobi Ninja in the first place.

While the myth that Ninja were birthed in the deep forests—spawned from "demons"!—is not without a smattering of fact, the greatest factual influence on the rise of Japanese Ninja was the existence of a similar—highly successful—cadre that had already been operating in China for centuries.

Moshuh Nanren: Chinese Ninja

It's no secret Japan "borrowed" much of its initial culture from China. Consequently, it's not surprising to discover that much of the strategy, tactics, and techniques used by medieval Japanese Ninja had its origins in China.

China possesses a long and bloody history of espionage and assassination. Never was this more true than during what is known as the Warring States Period (453–221 B.C.E.), a turbulent time that saw the rise of military geniuses such as Sun Tzu.

The very vastness of the Chinese realm demanded that the Emperor, his ministers, and indeed anyone who was anyone or who harbored any ambitions of ever becoming anyone field their own effective cadre and corps of masterful espionage operatives.

By necessity and nature, the most accomplished of these agents, assassins, and spies have remained hidden—perhaps forever lost—to history, unknown to us—a lasting testament to their shadow craft. However, we do know about one highly effective group of semi-mythical assassin spies who occupied more or less the same darkened spot in Imperial Chinese society that the Shinobi warriors would later come to fill in medieval Japan.

Briefly, the *Moshuh Nanren* was a league of espionage agents and secret society members who operated in China before the first century of the Common Era.

Moshuh Nanren were espionage experts commissioned to spy and carry out selective assassinations for the Imperial Chinese court. Greatly feared by the common people, Moshuh Nanren were part Gestapo/part Special Forces, their mandate and mission was to quell potential dissent by cutting off the head (often literally!) of any would-be reform, rebellion, or religious group daring to disturb the "harmony" of the Dragon Throne.

Like any state police/counterterrorist/"death squad," Moshuh Nanren used (counter) terror against anyone threatening the Imperial court.

4. Moshuh-Nanren, Chinese "ninja"

Fear was their greatest weapon. Opponents disappeared in the middle of the night. When their bodies were discovered days later, a look of horror would be on the face of the victim, yet *no marks* would be found on the body! And so the rumor spread of the supernatural killing abilities of Moshuh Nanren—the ability to kill with just a touch (see *the Fifth Hall: Specialized Combat Training Touch*).

An enemy's fears and superstitions are always a potent weapon to use against that enemy, and Moshuh Nanren did all they could to encourage such fear and superstition in their targets. Thus, to add to this fear, disinformation was circulated that the Moshuh Nanren were descended from mythical forest demons known as *Lin Kuei* (Lin Kway), just as similar propaganda would be spread by the later Japanese Shinobi of their descent from Tengu, the mythical forest demons of Japan.

Imperial-sanctioned Moshuh Nanren existed in one form or another for centuries serving the various dynasties of emperors of China.

But whenever a new Emperor took the throne, he would purge those in the court thought loyal to the previous Emperor, including not just ministers but also the former Emperor's spies and executioners.

As a result, eventually the techniques of the Moshuh Nanren, as well as the displaced assassins themselves, began to filter out into Chinese society itself.

These disinfranchised Moshuh Nanren sometimes founded secret societies (similar to the ones they had originally been sanctioned to fight) and carried on political or criminal activities against the new dynasty.

Other Moshuh Nanren became criminals and/or hired themselves and their considerable spying and slaying skills out to the highest bidder.

Some of the more effective Moshuh Nanren strategies and techniques—killing techniques—were eventually incorporated into the mainstream Chinese *Wu Shu Kung-Fu* (martial arts).

Likewise, Moshuh Nanren are credited with influencing the development of both the *Hwang-Do* warriors of Korea and, as we will see shortly, the Shinobi Ninja of Japan.

Indeed, the interchange between many such Eastern killer cadre, criminal organizations, and secret societies goes much deeper than unstudied Westerners might at first suspect.

The First Ninja

Moshuh Nanren techniques from China began filtering into Japan between the first and fifth centuries C.E.

The actual term "ninja" and the first Japanese warrior who could rightfully be called "ninja" appeared in the sixth century C.E. during Japan's bloody Skotoku War of succession.

When the Japanese Emperor Yomei died, a war of succession broke out between the rightful Prince Skotoku and ambitious members of the Moriya clan.

Prince Shotoku was fighting a losing battle—literally—until he was saved by a mysterious warrior-monk named *Otomo-No-Saijin*.

Otomo's keen insights and penetrating intelligence cut to the heart of Shotoku's problems and, by listening to Otomo's advice, Prince Shotoku was able to make short work and sushi of his enemies.

Once he took the throne, Shotoku repaid Otomo by making him a combination Imperial adviser and head of the Imperial bodyguard. Otomo then used his expertise at spying to quell any possible threats to Shotoku's rule.

Early on, Prince Shotoku gave Otomo the codename *"Shinobi,"* literally "Sneaky one" or, more properly, "He who enters by stealth."

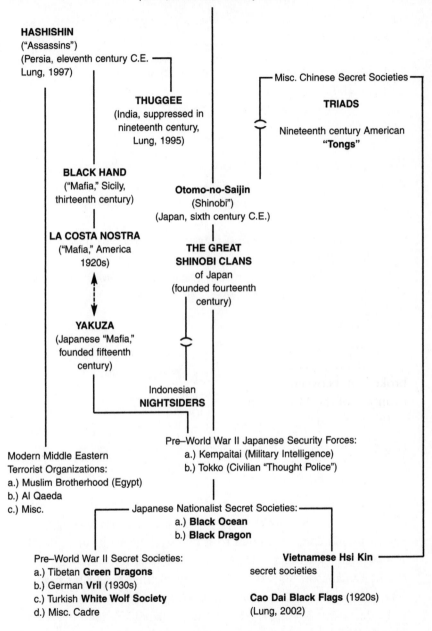

MOSHUH NANREN
(China, before sixth century B.C.E.

HASHISHIN
("Assassins")
(Persia, eleventh century C.E.
Lung, 1997)

Misc. Chinese Secret Societies

THUGGEE
(India, suppressed in
nineteenth century,
Lung, 1995)

TRIADS

Nineteenth century American
"Tongs"

BLACK HAND
("Mafia," Sicily,
thirteenth century)

Otomo-no-Saijin
(Shinobi")
(Japan, sixth century C.E.)

LA COSTA NOSTRA
("Mafia," America
1920s)

**THE GREAT
SHINOBI CLANS**
of Japan
(founded fourteenth
century)

YAKUZA
(Japanese "Mafia,"
founded fifteenth
century)

Indonesian
NIGHTSIDERS

Modern Middle Eastern
Terrorist Organizations:
a.) Muslim Brotherhood (Egypt)
b.) Al Qaeda
c.) Misc.

Pre–World War II Japanese Security Forces:
a.) Kempaitai (Military Intelligence)
b.) Tokko (Civilian "Thought Police")

Japanese Nationalist Secret Societies:
a.) **Black Ocean**
b.) **Black Dragon**

Pre–World War II Secret Societies:
a.) Tibetan **Green Dragons**
b.) German **Vril** (1930s)
c.) Turkish **White Wolf Society**
d.) Misc. Cadre

Vietnamese Hsi Kin

secret societies

Cao Dai Black Flags (1920s)
(Lung, 2002)

5. "The Ninja Connection"?

FYI: The word "ninja" comes from the Japanese writing *(kanji)* of Shinobi and is made up of two parts: the first part meaning "spirit," the second part meaning "edge."

Where "Shinobi" Otomo learned his espionage skills isn't known for certain, though it does not take a great leap of the imagination to figure out Otomo had somehow learned the skills and skulduggery of the Moshuh Nanren.

Some speculate that Otomo may have been a Moshuh Nanren agent himself!

Whichever side he was ultimately playing for, Otomo aka Shinobi rightfully deserves the title "Japan's first *ninja.*"

Mad Monks

Otomo-Shinobi was a *yamabushi* (lit. "mountain warrior"). Yamabushi (aka sohei) were Buddhist monks who established fortress-like monastaries on secluded mountains.

While Otomo and his patron Shotoku lived, these monasteries enjoyed the blessing of the powers that be. However, when these two patrons passed from the scene, jealous and fearful Samurai lords *(Daimyo)* and court intriguers began plotting against these religious strongholds.

As internecine warfare increased between rival Samurai factions and families at the Royal Court vying for oneupmanship, Yamabushi monasteries continued to grow, swelling with unemployed *Ronin* Samurai, general malcontents, and "political outlaws." As a result, Yamabushi "monks" spent as much time practicing martial arts and plotting coup as they did reading Buddhist sutra.

In this way they were similar to the (in)famous Shaolin monks of Hunan, China (see Lung, forthcoming).

It is important at this point to understand how Buddhism, particularly Chinese Buddhism, played a major role in the emergence of the Shinobi Ninja in Japan.

Buddhism arrived in Japan around 586 C.E. The Yamoto Emperor at the time was so impressed he sent groups of students to China to study Buddhism in depth.

It's hard to believe Chinese officials would pass up such a golden opportunity to infiltrate Moshuh Nanren operatives into these returning students and/or otherwise subvert more than one of these students into becoming double agents.

Perhaps this is where Otomo-no-Saijin learned his "ninja" (i.e., Moshuh Nanren) skills?

Shotoku's patronage and conversion to Otomo-Shinobi's Yamabushi/Buddhism religion angered many in Japan.

Up until the coming of Buddhism, "Animism" (the belief all things contain an "animating" spirit) was the major influence on Japanese religious thought.

The indigenous *Ainu* practiced a form of this belief (see *White Samurai,* below). The rest of Japan also practiced a more complicated form of animist/ancestor worship later systemized as the religion of Shinto ("Way of the Gods").

Buddhism pissed off many Japanese, especially Samurai, who felt that the religion didn't give sufficient homage to Japanese ancestors and cultural heroes. Some resented Buddhism simply because it was foreign.

After Shotoku and Otomo, succeeding Emperors—often under pressure from militant Samurai Daimyo—began openly persecuting Buddhists in general and the Yamabushi in particular.

But, by the beginning of the Heian period (794–1194 C.E.), Buddhism in Japan had already established itself as a religious "force" to be reckoned with.

By this time, the Yamabushi had developed into a fighting force to rival even the great clans of Samurai. Up till this time, the only thing that had kept Samurai Daimyo from turning on the Yamabushi was the fact the various Samurai clans were not united under one banner and instead squandered their resources fighting among themselves.

However, after the death of Shotoku, large-scale fighting broke out between the followers of Shinto and the followers of Buddhism; with the Japanese ruling class and Samurai supporting Shinto, and the lower classes and Yamabushi embracing Buddhism.

A Yamabushi named En-No-Gyoja tried to bring peace to the warring factions by creating a new "religion," blending what he felt was the best of Shintoism with Buddhism, to create *Shugendo* ("The Way of Spiritual Power"). Of course, this only pissed off Shinto traditionalists even more.

Thus, as this new Shugendo religion took root and gained in popularity with the common folk, the ruling class began a pogrom to wipe out Shugendo followers.

In the chaos and slaughter that followed, many temples *(ji)* and monasteries, including Buddhist temples not affiliated with Shugendo, were burned to the ground.

Those Yamabushi not killed outright were hunted down and slaughtered.

But some of these Yamabushi survived and went underground, hiding out under the guise of farmers, tradesmen, even priests in accepted religious sects.

Many of these "Yamabushi-turned-farmers" settled in and around Iga and Koga provinces in central Japan. Not surprising, this area would later become a major staging ground for the great medieval Shinobi Ninja clans—direct descendants of these displaced Yamabushi.

The "Peaceful" Period

This is a very misnamed period in Japanese history.

It was during this *Heian* (so-called peaceful) period that we witness the rise of the great Samurai clans, privileged families that would eventually place power into the hands of the first *Shogun* (supreme warlord).

To regress: In 645, a palace coup brought about *by students who had studied in China* assassinated the Imperial heir-apparent and placed a senile puppet emperor on the throne.*

Behind this black curtain of intrigue and insurgency, a mysterious master-puppeteer named Lord Kamatori was pulling the strings.

To give the devil his due, Kamatori ultimately helped centralize rule in Japan, welding contentious clans of warring, autonomous Samurai into something close to an Imperial state, at least to all outward appearances, a state ruled by the Emperor—aged and decrepit though he was.

Kamatori's Imperial unification efforts gave this period in Japanese history the name "Heian" though, in actuality, it was anything but.

———————

Under Imperial decree, all lands in Japan were declared to be the sole property of the Emperor, to be administered by his appointed governors. From now on Samurai lords, the Daimyo, were merely to "oversee" the care and development of lands they once claimed as their own, and on which they had based their fortunes and futures and, in many instances, had literally invested the sweat, blood, and tears of their entire clans.

Outraged by this blatant land seizure and in defiance, Daimyo began "donating" their lands to nearby Buddhist temples and monasteries. In return, the temples and monasteries allowed the donator to remain on the land as an "overseer"—working and car-

———

*Was this the hand of Moshuh Nanren agents at work?

ing for it, so long as a yearly "donation" of rice was made to the particular temple who "owned" the land.

All lands owned by these temples and monasteries was, of course, exempt from taxation by the Imperial government and, needless to say, the amount of "donation" a Daimyo and his clan had to make each year to their respective temple was considerably less than the "tax" the owner-turned-caretaker would have to pay the Imperial court and the self-serving vultures who roosted there.

Not surprising, this "arrangement" between Daimyo and Abbott angered the Imperial court and its money-grubbing ministers and brought even more persecution down on the heads of Buddhists in general and the Samurai "tax evaders" in particular.

These troubling times increased the influx of both social exiles and economic expatriates, both of whom would soon swell the ranks of the great Ninja clans.

Economic hard times forced Daimyo to downsize their retinue and cut back on the number of Samurai they kept under arms.

These suddenly out-of-work Samurai were known as *Ronin* (lit. "Wave men," that is, men cast about by fate like leaves on an ocean).

Ronin are to Japan what cowboys—outlaws in particular—are to America.

The most famous group of celebrated Ronin are *"The 47 Ronin"* (see Lung and Prowant, 2001:38).

Some Ronin hung up their swords (but always within reach!) and became farmers. Others joined monks' orders like the Yamabushi, acting as both bodyguards and martial arts instructors, ever honing their skills and those of their students for the day their swords would once again be in demand.

They wouldn't have long to wait.

Still other Ronin became out-and-out criminals. In fact, it is this peaceful (Heian) period that saw the emergence of the secretive "ninja" criminal brotherhood that later become the Japanese "Mafia," the *Yakuza*.

By the end of the twelfth century, the end of the Heian period, all the players were in place for an event that would set the standard for the next 650 years of Japanese history, 650 years during which Ninja would flourish!

Scourge of the Shoguns

Once all the land was placed under control of the Imperial court to dole out as the Emperor (actually self-serving ministers and courtiers) saw fit, in effect consolidating power into the hands of a few, this inadvertently led to the rise of the great Samurai families of Japan: Taira, Genji (Minimoto), and Fujiwara.

These great families fought for the upper hand over one another—first secretly, behind the black curtain of innuendo and intrigue—and then openly.

Savage civil war erupted at the beginning of the twelfth century between the Taira and Minimoto clans. This initial clash led to the almost total annihilation of both clans.

However, by the end of the twelfth century, the Minimoto under the warlord Yoritomo had rallied, regrouped, and rearmed. When the dust from "round two" finally settled, the house of Taira had fallen and Minimoto Yoritomo had emerged as the de facto ruler of Japan—its first Shogun.

Thus, the Heian period gave way to the "Kamakura" period in Japanese history, so-called for the city where Yoritomo established his capital.

More important, Yoritomo had established a line of Shoguns (military leaders) who would hold sway over the isles of Japan for the next 650 years.

"It is believing steadfastly that we shall attain the highest power, that we shall acquire the qualities that make a man almost more than man, since they allow him to govern and subdue those by whom he is surrounded." (Yoritomo, quoted in *Influence: How to Exert It*, Kessinger Publications Co. 1916:43)

WHITE SAMURAI

One main reason for Yoritomo's victory over the Taira was the fact he recruited *Ainu* into his ranks.

The Ainu are the indigenous Caucasians who inhabited the islands of Japan long before the ancestors of the present-day Sino-Japanese (known as *Yayoi*) invaded the islands around 300 B.C.E. from China and/or the Korean Peninsula.

The Ainu (the word means "Hairy Ones") swelled Yoritomo's ranks, fought with distinction, and much to the chagrin of the xenophobic Japanese, Yoritomo even "knighted" several Ainu as Samurai.

Even today, modern Japanese would rather not be reminded that their pure bloodline has Caucasian-Ainu hemoglobin pumping through it!

Some experts have even speculated that the distinctive elevated noses, flatter cheeks, pointed chins, and lighter skin indicative of the present-day Japanese Imperial family are all DNA heirlooms from Ainu ancestors.

This Ainu connection is important because the superstition and shamanistic practices of these Ainu became an important factor in the development of the Shinobi mystical practices in general and the Ninth Hall of Ninjutsu mastery in particular (see The Ninth Hall: The Art of Mysticism).

Using Ainu warriors to augment his forces was probably Yoritomo's smartest move.

His dumbest move was to try and kill his brother, Yoshitsune.

YOSHITSUNE

After the initial defeat of Minimoto by the Taira, Yoritomo's younger brother, Yoshitsune (aka Ushiwara), then but a child, was hidden in the monastery near the Yamabushi stronghold on Mt. Hei, where he trained for the day his clan would rise again.

Here fact blurs with fiction.

Legends tell how young Yoshitsune would sneak out of the monastery to learn martial arts from those mysterious half-man, half-bird demons known as *Tengu* (see section *Gods and Goblins).*

Truth be known, this is a thinly disguised version of the less-palatable truth: that the only folk who would dare defy the Emperor's court and risk the wrath of the powerful Taira clan by hiding out the Taira's blood enemies were *Ninja.*

The bottom line of the story? Yoshitsune and Yoritomo first crossed racial lines by enlisting the aid of the "barbarian" Ainu, before then compounding their affront to proper Japanese etiquette by crossing social lines to enlist the aid of despised "ninja" to defeat their enemies.*

It is understandable that "proper" Japanese history should shroud this period of their violent history with myth, especially when it comes to the part pariahs like "ninja" played in the creation of a unified Japan.

Ninja have never been popular in Japan, and the idea that the first Shogun should have to resort to knighting the "subhuman" Ainu and, worse yet, should soil his honor by gallivanting around with back-stabbing assassins, is just too much for most Japanese purists to admit—at least openly.

---

*In Japanese, this is called *Masakatsu,* lit. "Victory by any means necessary." In other words, the winners are the ones who write the history books!

———

From contested fiction to undisputed fact: no sooner had Yoritomo seized power than he began disposing of any—real or imagined—present, past, and possibly future threat to his rule.

This included not only old political rivals but also members of his own family . . . with the very popular Yoshitsune topping his hit list.

But Yoshitsune had learned his "Ninja" lessons well and vanished just ahead of the killers sent by his brother.

———

Japanese myth is filled to overflowing with stories of Yoshitsune. Admittedly Japan's most popular folk hero, not surprising, there are several different endings to the Yoshitsune legend:

One ending has Yoshitsune secretly beheaded and buried by his brother's henchmen.

Tale two has Yoshitsune committing *hari-kiri* rather than be captured.

The legends of the Shinobi realm tell a different ending.

Among the Shinobi, Yoshitsune—whom they call Ushiwara—not only escaped his brother's wrath but also founded the *Karama-Hachi-Ryu* school of Ninjutsu.

FYI: It is a well-established fact that Yoshitsune taught Minimoto troops "unconventional" (i.e., *ninja!*) techniques that helped lead ultimately to the Minimoto triumph.

Before their second confrontation with the Taira, Minimoto forces were required to study these Ninja covert operations, strategy, tactics, and techniques and that this is what turned the tide against the Taira.

———

As for Yoshitsune's brother, Yoritomo died in 1198 after being thrown from his horse.

To his final breath, the first Shogun swore he'd been attacked by the spirit (*kami*) of his missing brother, Yoshitsune, that had suddenly appeared in front of the horse, causing it to bolt.

The Shinobi version? The very-much still alive Yoshitsune disguised himself to appear as a ghost to frighten Yoritomo to death, a technique known as *Kyonin-No-Jutsu*, "Taking advantage of the fears and superstitions of an enemy."

THE GREAT CLANS

Ninjutsu as an art came into its own following the emergence of the great Shinobi Ninja clans in the thirteenth century. These clans included the *Hattori,* the *Momochi,* and the *Oe.* The groundwork for these clans had already been set in place by the end of the twelfth century.

Thus, as Japan moved into the thirteenth century, scores of Shinobi clans collectively held sway in the provinces of Iga and Koga.

Any Samurai wishing to pass through these lands did so at great personal risk. Any Daimyo entering this region had to do so with a large company of troops, or only after he had petitioned the local Ninja *Jonin* (Chiefs) with generous "tribute." (Think Robin Hood and Sherwood Forest . . . or, better yet, Cu Chi, Vietnam!)

For example, Iga province was ruled jointly by the Hattori and Oe clans. Over in Koga province, over fifty Ninja families exerted control.

Some of these Ninja clans were rivals and kept up ongoing feuds that would be the envy of any Hatfield or McCoy!

Still other clans were formed by Ronin seeking to destroy the Iga Ninja.

The fierce infighting and jockeying for position constantly going on between rival Samurai Daimyo provided a lot of work for the Ninja, helping the Shinobi to hone his deadly skills to an even keener edge.

By the fourteenth century, Japanese were again fighting what amounted to civil war between Samurai lords in the north and their rivals in the south. This internecine Samurai slaughter provided a fertile field for the Ninja "farmers" of Iga and Koga to sow further seeds of dissent between their foes.

Some of the Shinobi threw themselves in on the side of Samurai lords whose goals matched their own. Other Ninja clans simply sold themselves to the highest bidder.

Some clans played both ends against the middle, instigating as much ill will between Samurai lords as possible. The enemy of my enemy is my friend.

Some did this because it helped stimulate "business," while others did so simply because they knew so long as Samurai were busy butchering each other, they wouldn't have time to slaughter the poor, innocent "farmers" of Iga and Koga.

The fourteenth century saw a great increase in Ninja activity in and around Iga and Koga. The Hattori and Oe clans controlled the central part of Koga while the rival Momochi held sway in the southern part of the province. The fearsome Fijibayashi clan controlled a large part of northern Koga and a good piece of southern Iga. The rest of Iga was under the influence of the *Kusunoki-Ryu,* a Ninja school founded by the (in)famous Ronin warrior Massashige Kunsunoki.

Despite the fact that their clans were blood enemies, some historians have speculated that Sandayu Mososhi, Jonin of the Mososhi clan, and Nagato Fujibayashi, leader of the Fijibayashi Ninja were, in fact, *the same man!*

When you learn a little more about the Sixth Hall, "The Art of Disguise," you'll realize this is not too far-fetched since it is theo-

The Great Clans
Hattori
Momochi
Fijibayashi
Oe
Mososhi
over fifty total

(to Russia)

Hokkaido

(to Korea)

Kyoto

Edo
(modern Tokyo)

(to China)

Mt. Fuji

Honshu

Shikoku

Kyushu

6. Medieval Shinobi Ninja Clans

rized that some Jonin maintained upward of *three* complete families, with three completely separate identities, to keep ahead of
Samurai death squads and rival ninja assassins.

So long as Samurai were busy killing each other, they were too busy
to try stamping out and curbing the growing power of the Shinobi.

All this was soon to change!

WARLORDS AND SHADOW-WARRIORS

In 1586, Oda Nobunaga seized control of the Imperial court
and the Shogunal courts at Kyoto along with help from his two
generals, Ieyasu Tokugawa and Hideyoshi Toyotomi.

When the smoke finally cleared and heads were counted (literally!), though there were still Samurai lords who defied him, Oda
was, de facto, the ruler of Japan.

Oda, Tokugawa, and Toyotomi had only two things in common:
one was their power lust. The second, their hatred for Buddhism.

Immediately after seizing power, Oda set his sights on every
Buddhist in Japan. As a result, the Shinobi Ninja of Iga and Koga
became Oda's sworn enemies.

Recall that the Shinobi Ninja were mostly followers of the *Shin-
gon* and *Tendai* sects of Buddhism, sects who refused to acknowl-
edge Oda's power and, instead, threw in with his detractors. In
retaliation, Oda launched several large "search and destroy" missions into Iga and Koga provinces, thinking to break the back of
the great Shinobi clans. However, like similar efforts undertaken
by U.S. forces fighting the Vietnam War centuries later, all these
missions succeeded in doing was (1) destroying the homes and vil-
lages of the few legit farmers in Iga and Koga, while (2) getting a
whole lot of Oda's own troops killed via strategically placed booby-
traps and well-aimed *shuriken* in the back!

Oda eventually succeeded in destroying the military power of
the great Tendai rebel stronghold on Mt. Hiri as well as the other

monasteries that had defied him. But in the long run, all this accomplished was to help swell Ninja ranks with even more displaced, pissed off priests and Yamabushi.

Over the years, attempts were made by Ninja on the life of Oda, but all failed.

One of the more ingenious attempts made on Oda's life was made by the Ninja *chunin* Goemon Ishikawa.

Goemon succeeded in gaining entrance to Oda's sleeping quarters, where he then hid for days in the rafters above Oda's sleeping mat, patiently waiting for the Shogun's return.

This technique is known as *Tsuchiguno* (lit. "Bat hangs in the rafters"), simply put, waiting for an enemy in a place you know he will eventually come to.

Myamoto Musashi once used this same ploy when challeged to duel a group of brothers. Arriving at the appointed spot an hour ahead of time, Musashi hid himself in a tree. When the brothers arrived, they found no Musashi, so they eventually settled down to lounging and then drinking.

Musashi waited patiently until all the brothers were either asleep or drunk before leaping out of hiding to slay them all!

When Oda finally returned and went to sleep, Goemon ran a piece of thread down to Oda's lips to drip poison down the thread into the sleeping man's mouth.

Unfortunately, as far as Ishikawa's prospects for a long life were concerned, the ploy was discovered before it had a chance to succeed.

FYI: If this ploy sounds familiar, you may have seen it portrayed in the 1967 James Bond film *You Only Live Twice*.

Finally, in 1582 Oda Nobunaga was assassinated by one of his own minor lords.

However, Shinobi lore confides that this betraying lord, Akechi by name, was under the control and influence of Jonin Sandayu Nagato of the Fujibayashi clan. Sandayu, having himself only barely escaped the Oda-sanctioned conflagration of Iga and Koga that had claimed so many of his family and Shinobi brothers, had finally gotten his revenge.

Still another version has Oda finally betrayed by Toyotomi, his "faithful" general.

The Taiko. With the death of Oda Nobunaga, his general and closest confidant, Hideyoshi Toyotomi took power.

Hideyoshi truly stands alone of all warlords in Japan's long and bloody history.

By 1590, having successfully outmaneuvered all other contenders, Toyotomi finally succeeded in doing what no one before him had done: unify all of Japan under one iron fist.

What makes this accomplishment all the more amazing is the fact that Hideyoshi wasn't even a Samurai, instead, he'd paid his dues and had gotten his the hard way, by clawing his way up from poverty and obscurity to become the most powerful man in Japan.

What helped Toyotomi attain such heights? Ruthlessness, craft, and cunning.

And, oh yeah, the fact that he was *ninja* probably helped!

————

Hideyoshi Toyotomi was born in 1536 into a family of commoners. There was little to distinguish this pale, sickly boy from his peers— nothing to indicate that he would one day become "Supreme Leader" (*Taiko*) of Japan, whose armies would one day be pounding at the gates of both China and Korea.

While still a boy, Hideyoshi was expelled from a Buddhist school for destroying an image of the Buddha. This humiliation and punishment may help explain his lifelong vendetta against Buddhism.

Exiled and shamed by this expulsion, Hideyoshi soon fell in with a cutthroat band of "ninja" thieves and highwaymen. From these Fagin-like mentors, Hideyoshi learned covert techniques and spying tricks that would later aid his rise to power.

As he grew older, Hideyoshi became an expert at stealth, specializing in robbing the homes of wealthy Japanese, often getting a job as a servant to "case the joint" beforehand.

During one such infiltration, Hideyoshi chanced to meet Lord Oda Nobunaga and overhear Oda talking strategy with his host.

When Oda voiced concern over an upcoming military campaign, young Hideyoshi broke all protocol—risking death—to offer Oda a heretofore unknown but vital piece of intelligence about Oda's enemy.

Impressed as much with the information (which later proved true and helped Oda win the battle) as with the boldness of the young Hideyoshi, Oda enlisted the youth as a spy.

Before long, Toyotomi was made first an officer, then a general.

In short order, Hideyoshi had become Oda's right-hand man, displacing many of Oda's longtime associates—earning himself many dangerous enemies.

Soon, Toyotomi's access to the Shogun's ear was challenged only by the equally ambitious Ieyasu Tokugawa, who feared Hideyoshi's ninja talents and the young general's growing spy network enough to wait his turn at power.

———————————————

During his service to Oda, Hideyoshi used his well-developed network of assassins and spies to gather information and dispatch anyone he thought might threaten Oda's rule . . . and his own future plans.

Later, he would use this same league of "ninja" to first consolidate and then continue his own rule.

———————

Some have speculated that Hideyoshi might have actually been a Ninja plant—a sleeper agent—assigned to burrow as deep into the confidence of Oda Nobunaga as possible, feeding information to his Jonin controllers and disinformation to Oda, until the day his masters sent word that Oda was to be assassinated.

If true, Hideyoshi obviously turned on his Jonin controllers at some point after gaining power, pursuing a relentless policy of slaughter against his former trainers; a ruthless campaign of slaughter fueled by both fear and common sense. In other words, if the plant theory was true, Hideyoshi was anxious to destroy his controllers before they could get their revenge against their renegade agent.

Whatever the truth, Hideyoshi died in his sleep, an old man, at the ripe age of sixty-two in 1598, leaving behind few admirers and even fewer *living* enemies!

His skills had taken him far and served him well.

The Tokugawa. With the death of Hideyoshi, Ieyasu Tokugawa took power. This marked the begining of a more than 250-year rule by the Tokugawa clan.

On the positive side, this Tokugawa Period saw the systemization of the *Bushido,* the code of the Samurai.

Under the Tokugawa, Japan enjoyed relative peace for the first time in its history.

To his credit, Ieyasu did curtail his attacks on Buddhists, but only so he could concentrate his enmity toward crushing the encroaching *Christian* influence.

Initially, Taiko Hideyoshi had encouraged Christian missionaries, which he saw as a possible counter to the influence of Buddhism. That is, until Hideyoshi got back reports of how powerful and controlling the Christian church and its priests were in Europe.

Too late. In 1597, Hideyoshi had issued anti-Christian decrees and, when these failed to stem the church's growth, he began openly persecuting Japanese Christians and their European masters as vehemently as he had previously hunted Buddhists.

The Tokugawa Shogunate continued with this paranoia and persecution by issuing in 1614 an edict forbidding the practice of Christianity in Japan altogether.

Too little, too late.

After the death of Ieyasu, his grandson Iyemitsu continued the Tokugawa's anti-Christian stance. In 1638, Iyemitsu used Ninja sappers to help him infiltrate and destroy the heavily defended enclave of 38,000 Christians at Shimbara, slaughtering all but 105.

Unfortunately, as far as the Ninja "business" was concerned, the rise of the Tokugawa regime meant the end to most of the petty—albeit profitable—wars between rival Samurai Daimyo and spelled the end to the Shinobi Ninja's favorite sport: playing one Samurai lord off against the other, thereby keeping their foes constantly at one anothers' throat!

Yet while the rise of the Tokugawa and their sword-imposed peace severely cut into Ninja business, the Tokugawa themselves were not shy about hiring Ninja for espionage and even assassination—activities "proper" Samurai like the Tokugawa couldn't possibly involve themselves in.

Obviously, Iyemitsu had learned valuable lessons from his wily grandfather, the ever-patient Ieyesu. Had Ieyasu Tokugawa directly challenged the rise of Hideyoshi, it is doubtful the Tokugawa patriarch would have lived to become the Shogun of Japan. As it was, Ieyasu respected, that is, *feared* Hideyoshi's Ninja prowess and his formidable spy network enough to bide his time.

Evidently, Ieyasu Tokugawa realized early on that he would not be able to counter Hideyoshi's growing influence and that if he hoped to survive and not "disappear" as so many of Hideyoshi's detractors seemed to have a habit of doing, the Tokugawa would need to get their own "ninja."

Above all else, Ieyasu realized the importance of maintaining a strong cadre of spies himself, having seen firsthand how easily Ninja could subvert even a trusted associate—for example, the ease in which the Ninja-inspired Lord Akechi assassinated Oda Nobunaga. To prevent this happening to himself, Ieyesu contracted Ninja "bodyguards" from the warriors of the Hattori clan. Ieyasu even appointed Ninja Jonin Hanzo Hattori to his staff of advisers and surrounded himself with an impenetrable wall of Ninja "gardeners" and "servants."

FYI: Proper Japanese etiquette still required Ieyasu to maintain the facade of his Ninja being "gardeners" and "servants" for him to avoid affronting the Bushido code that still scorned the Ninja's direct—*realistic!*—methods of removing enemies.

———

With the enforced ban on slaughter between Samurai because of the Tokugawa-inspired peace, many Ninja clans simply faded into obscurity due to "unemployment," that is, lack of a worthy enemy to keep them sharp.

Other "ninja," individuals and whole clans, turned (back) to crime.

Yet even in such lean times, there were a few Ninja who still managed to prosper.

For example, the Hattori continued expanding their "bodyguards" service and eventually helped form the nucleus for the modern Japanese criminal police.

Ironically, by the beginning of the twentieth century, you had *Yakuza,* so-called Japanese "Mafia" gangsters who traced themselves back to "ninja" criminal cadre, playing cat and mouse with

Japanese police, who could also claim descent from Ninja clans such as the Hattori!

After all, Ninja are nothing if not adaptable. Adapt or die has always been the favored Ninja mantra.

Modern-Day Ninja

In 1854, Commodore Matthew Perry sailed into Tokyo Bay demanding that Japan open its ports to trade with the West, effectively ending hundreds of years of Japanese isolationism.

This event also heralded a new era in "ninja" operations.

"Ninja" were there at the beginning, a group of them having been hired to sneak aboard Perry's ships and gather information on these newly arrived *Gaijin* "barbarians."

These ninja spies had been contracted by concerned Samurai who saw the encroaching Westerners, Americans in particular, as a threat to traditional Japanese culture.

Thirteen years later, in 1867, some of these idealistic—albeit impatient—Samurai succeeded in overthrowing the last of the Tokugawa, replacing this lineage of Shoguns with a stronger Imperial rule they hoped would present a unified force against the kind of foreign domination suffered by such countries as China and Vietnam (Lung, 2003).

A decade later, in 1877, what would be the last great Samurai revolt—seeking to reestablish Samurai feudalism—failed. As a consequence, the Samurai class was officially abolished.

But the Samurai have a saying (stolen from the Ninja!): "Nine times down, ten times up!"

Hoping to someday regain their lost status, while in the meantime pledging themselves to safeguard Japan from foreign control, some of these newly dispossessed Samurai formed themselves into nationalist secret societies.

BEHIND THE BLACK CURTAIN

Necessity being the stepmother of conspiracy, these nineteenth-century Samurai secret societies either recruited veteran ninja to do their dark bidding, or else created and trained their own cadre of agents whose mandate was to ferret out intelligence and, when need be, carry out assassinations both inside Japan and overseas.

The more successful of these secret societies were bankrolled by rich and powerful Samurai families who controlled Japan's growing military-industrial complex.

Collectively, these influential families were/*are* known as the *Zaibatsu*.

The Zaibatsu was closely allied with the Japanese military and thus with the military's intelligence bureau, the much feared *Kempeitai*.

Kempeitai operatives were "ninja" in the traditional sense of the word, carrying out intelligence gathering, assassination, and general skullduggery wherever Japanese interests—and *ambitions!*—were involved.

The Kempeitai was literally a two-edged sword—equally keen at cutting down real and imagined foes of Japan both inside Japan and abroad.

So closely intertwined were these nationalist secret societies and cliques that it is impossible to say where one left off and the other began. In fact, one man might belong to several different, yet interconnected, groups.

For example, an influential Yakuza headman, a *Kuromaku* (lit. "Black Curtain") might belong to the same nationalist secret society as the police detective assigned to investigate him. These two would, in turn, hobnob with generals, and/or with members of the Kempeitai—all united by their rabid nationalism . . . and *ambition!*

Some of these conspirators went so far as to feign hatred of one another when meeting in public and political circles, all the while plotting together behind closed doors.

These secret societies not only practiced their schemes in the streets of Tokyo but also fielded agents and front-operations abroad.

Some of these overseas agents worked for the military, spying out potential military threats and probing for weaknesses in potential soon-to-be enemies.

Still other agents worked for Zaibatsu concerns, infiltrating rival foreign companies and corporations, stealing industrial secrets, sabotaging rival businesses, and helping Japanese companies keep a leg up on the competition.

Other secret societies infiltrated agents into religious groups, student unions, and even martial arts clubs, both inside Japan and abroad.

By far, the most effective—thus the most *feared*—of these secret societies were the *Black Ocean Society* (founded 1881) and the *Black Dragon Society* (founded 1901).

THE BLACK DRAGONS

The *Genyoshakai,* "the Black Ocean Society" in English, was founded by wealthy Samurai-turned-businessman Kotaro Hiraoka.

Originating in Kyushu province in Japan, this shadowy brotherhood soon spread throughout Japan. Having accomplished this, the Black Ocean then began sending agents overseas. It also began recruiting turncoats in foreign countries to spy and exert influence as far afield as China, Korea, Manchuria, Russia, and Indochina.

In short order, the Black Ocean became the consummate school for spies, adroit at gathering intelligence—domestic and foreign— as well as being masters at manipulating human frailty. The Black Ocean thus set the standard for many of the twentieth century's "spooks," for example, MI-6, OSS, KGB, CIA, and NSA.

In many ways foreshadowing a modern Al Qaeda terrorist network, the Black Ocean was also the twentieth century's first truly *international* terrorist organization—perhaps the first really effective international operation since the medieval Assassins cult.

Both inside Japan and abroad, Black Ocean operatives infiltrated religious groups, academic institutions, and already-existing secret societies.

Where easily infiltrated businesses and organizations were not already in place, Black Ocean "ninja" set up "false front" organizations and businesses designed not only to operate secretely "behind enemy lines" but also to recruit traitors from among the "enemy" population. "When my foe sends spies to pry into my affairs, I bribe them with lavish gifts, turning them around and making them into agents of my will" (Li Ch'uan, eighth century).

The Black Ocean was especially active in gathering information and extending its influence into Manchuria, where the founder Kotaro Hiraoka owned large tracts of mining land.

So successful was the Black Ocean Society that it spawned numerous imitators and offshoots.

The most (in)famous offshoot of the Black Ocean Society was the *Kokurkykai,* "the Black Dragon Society."

The Black Dragon was formed after evidence surfaced that Black Ocean "ninja" had been implicated in the assassination of Queen Min of Korea in 1895.

The Black Dragon Society, sometimes calling itself "the Amur Society," was founded in 1901, originally to carry out intelligence-gathering (and terrorism) operations inside Korea and China—both already targeted for eventual conquest by the Japanese Empire.

Founded by Kotaro Hiraoka's protégé Rychei Uchida, the Black Dragon's declared mission was to drive the Russians out of Manchuria, back across the Amur River (hence "the Amur Society"), which marks Manchuria's northern border with Russia.

The Black Dragon Society grew at a phenomenal rate and, in short order, had taken over most operations of the Black Ocean.

The Black Dragon soon became the most powerful secret society in Japan.

Some Black Dragon supporters were well known and some—including politicians—quite vocal in their support of Black Dragon aims, if not openly supporting their "questionable methods."

But, as behooves a "secret" society, most of Black Dragon's members remained hidden behind the black curtain.

Unlike the Black Ocean, who had had few qualms about initiating sundry thugs, known criminals, and killers into its ranks, the Black Dragon concentrated on recruiting young "clean-slate" students into its ranks—students who could be "molded," students eager to become *Soshi* (Jp. "Brave Knights") of the Black Dragon.

The *true* leaders of Japan, the Zaibatsu, who ran the military-industrial complex and financed both Black Ocean and now Black Dragon operations, already knew the value of having "ninja" in the right place at the right time.

During the Russo-Japanese War (1904–1905), Black Dragon "ninja" obtained detailed plans of the Russian naval installation at Port Arthur (Lu-shun, China), allowing the Japanese to stage a surprise attack and sink the Russian fleet.

FYI: Thirty-five years later, the Japanese would use this same tried-and-true "ninja" strategy at a place called Pearl Harbor!

Following their victory over the Russians, Japanese political and military leaders—many Black Dragon members themselves—began openly encouraging nationalist groups like the Black Dragon by pouring money (and manpower) into their overseas espionage operations. As a result, Black Dragon operations and "sleeper" cells were soon operating worldwide, from Manchuria to Indochina, from Hong Kong to the United States.

By the 1930s, evidence of Black Dragon influence was being felt as far afield as the United States, throughout the Caribbean, as well as in Africa and Turkey.

FYI: At its height in 1944, the Black Dragon would boast over 10,000 members!

Before World War II, the Black Dragon took deliberate steps to establish alliances with nationalist and fascist subversive groups worldwide. These included, but were by no means limited to, the nationalist *White Wolf Society* of Turkey and the *Hung* (Triads) Brotherhood of China and Hong Kong.

In anticipation of the 1940 Axis alliance, the Black Dragon entered into shadowy pacts with several "occult" secret societies in Italy and Germany, including the infamous *Thule Society* and the Aryan *Vril,* both of whose membership included prominent Nazis.

Closer to home in Asia, Black Dragon operatives continued infiltrating religious groups, secret societies, and fringe political groups, from Singapore, to Hong Kong, to mainland China.

One version of history has the Black Dragons *supporting* the overthrow of the Manchu (1911) and helping Sun-Yat-Sen to become China's first president.

Another version (or simple "phase two" of the same covert operation!) has the Black Dragons responsible for Sun-Yat-Sen's "untimely" death in 1925—his death helping plunge China into a decades-long civil war, *conveniently* weakening an already divided China and making China easy pickings for the coming Japanese invasion.

Through infiltration of Chinese secret societies, the Black Dragon was also able to establish a "fifth column" of secret supporters and subversives inside the British colony of Hong Kong in anticipation of Japan seizing that colony during World War II.

Likewise, Black Dragon operatives infiltrated key organizations—governmental posts, religious groups, disaffected political fringe groups, and already existing secret societies—in dozens of other Asian countries, including Vietnam.

―――――――

As in other parts of the world in general and Asia in particular, Black Dragon operatives burrowed their way into dozens of key organizations in Vietnam in anticipation of their wrenching control of colonial Indochina from the French during World War II.

Not only did Japanese agents infiltrate already existing Vietnamese *Hoi Kin* (lit. "secret societies") but also, where expedient, Japanese agents actually *founded* and funded several Vietnamese secret societies and religious fringe groups, many of which would later prove influential in the development of Vietnamese politics.

One of the best examples of Black Dragon "meddling" (i.e., infiltration and inciting) is evidence that they were instrumental in helping establish the *Cao Dai* religion in Vietnam in the 1920s. The Cao Dai, in turn, would be influential players in the political landscape of Vietnam for the next fifty years (see *Cao Dai Kung-Fu: Lost Fighting Arts of Vietnam* by Dr. Haha Lung. Loompanics Unlimited, 2003:20).

II. CRAFT AND TRAINING

⚡ ⚡

INTRODUCTION: *LOOKING FOR SIMILARITIES*

BEFORE WE SET OUT ON THE PATH THAT LEADS ever deeper into the Shinobi realm, we must first set our minds to looking for "similarities" of style, movement, and thinking. We must do this to avoid all seeming, petty, and often intentionally misleading "differences" designed to distract us from our purpose.

Some of these distractions—fake sign posts and faulty directions—were set up by the Shinobi themselves, those jealously guarding their time-honored secrets. Others are more contemporary stumbling blocks strung in our way by those motivated by enmity and envy or both.

At first glance, the Nine Halls appear to be vastly different from one another, both in what is studied in each and the primary approach to teaching/learning taken in each.

Yet, like so many things we will encounter during our sojourn through the Shinobi realm, this is but an illusion.

In seeking to master the teachings of the Ninja, we must seek out—and, once found, keep focused on—the "similarities."

For example, rather than allow ourselves to be dazzled by the seemingly hundreds of different kicks available to the novice martial artist, let us instead remind ourselves there are actually *only four* types of kicks in all martial arts.

Likewise, while the many "different" schools of warfare at first glance appear (and all claim) to have unique and "different" strategies for overcoming enemies, in actual fact, their "secret" strategies and "special" tactics are more similar to every other school than they are willing to admit (especially to themselves!).

Here lies the genius of such Masters as Sun Tzu and Miyamoto Musashi, both of whom built their strategies—still applicable today—on the singular insight that people are more alike than they are different.

Big surprise! We are more often defeated by tried-and-true plot and ploy than by untested poniard.

Thus, before crossing the threshold leading to that long corridor housing those foreboding, well-guarded nine portals of Ninja knowledge, we must first dedicate ourselves to understanding *the Three Types of "Craft"* and embrace the Shinobi's *Rules for Realistic Training,* and thereby *Developing Explosive Speed and Power,* time-honored Ninja methods—tactics, tools, and techniques—we can apply in *all* the Nine Halls.

The Three Types of "Craft"

People often speak of mastering the Ninja "Craft," that collective store of knowledge amassed over the centuries by Shinobi folk and their myriad imitators.

But, for a Ninja, "craft" has more than one meaning.

CRAFT AS VEHICLE

"Craft" is synonymous with a "vehicle" capable of taking us where we want to go, for example, an automobile that takes us down the the road, a boat taking us across a deep river, or a ship capable of sailing us safely across a dangerous, uncharted sea.

Ninjutsu, the "art" (jutsu) of the Ninja, is just such a "vehicle," one that is capable of taking us places we never imagined.

Simplistically, we set out to learn a few Ninja "tricks," perhaps to augment already existing martial arts skills. We might even bone up on some of the Ninja's techniques of burglary, pickpocketing, or disguise simply to pad our wallet. In these instances, Ninjutsu "takes us" where we want to go, that is, it gets the job done.

But for those few dedicated students who make mastery of Ninjutsu their life's work, the Nine Halls become *a solid framework,* around which there is no limit to what can be crafted. For such students, there is no limit to "where" and "how far" their Ninja Craft ("vehicle") can take them!

CRAFT AS SKILL

Over the centuries, medieval Shinobi folk, their descendants, and their myriad of imitators have amassed an incredible collection of knowledge—not just physical knowledge dealing with how to get over a castle wall and how to get over on an enemy, but knowledge ranging from how to use herbs to cure and kill, to psychological insights capable of instilling courage in brothers and inspiring fear in others!

This vast library of collective skills is "The Ninja Craft," a craft as intricate and as respected as any other workman's craft—the carpenter's craft, the mason's, the assassin's.

CRAFT AS STRATEGY

Finally, "craft" also means "cunning."

For Sun Tzu, the ultimate achievement was to defeat an enemy *without fighting.* Brain before bludgeon and blade.

This is also the ideal Lao Tzu set forth in the *Tao Te Ching,* dealing with a little problem *before* it gets to be a big problem.

Did someone say Hitler . . . Saddam Hussein . . . North Korea?

Thus, the ideal for the Ninja is to use strategy and cunning, that is, "craft," before having to resort to other more "stringent" Ninja "crafts."

"By learning do we teach. By teaching do we learn"
—Ninja adage

Rules for Realalistic Training

It is said: The more you sweat in times of peace the less you bleed in times of war.

Thus, we study the warrior masters of the past, to learn from their successes . . . to learn even more from their mistakes. We take these skills from the past and twist them to fit our needs—present and future.

But we need to constantly remind ourselves that this is not "back in the day," back when sword-wielding Samurai walked the land unchallenged . . . unchallenged that is, except for Ninja!

Technology-wise, *weapons*-wise, much has changed since those medieval times. Yet, predictably, the human animal has changed little. He is still driven by, and all too easily manipulated by, his hatreds, lusts, and fears.

Yet all too often it is not our fears and other emotions that lead us to ruin, rather it is our arrogance.

Back in those medieval times, a heavily armed Samurai finding himself confronted by a "peasant" or a "monk" armed only with a bamboo staff would snicker in contempt, knowing he already had this "battle" won. After all, what did a heavily armed Samurai have to fear from an unarmed peasant or monk?

Fast forward to today, and it's *you* being confronted by a knife-wielding thug. Like that Samurai of yore, you don't panic because you have a gun hidden inside your jacket.

But does this mean you're automatically going to survive this confrontation?

Theoretically, whoever gets to their weapon first will walk away the winner.

Don't bet your life on it.

In any "Dire-Threat-Situation" (DTS), especially a kill-or-be-killed confrontation involving weapons, you must *fight the man not the weapon*.

Whereas you can't break the metal barrel of the firearm pointing at you, you can smash the arm holding that weapon and, if need be, kill the brain sending signals to the trigger finger!

But how do you *realistically* train for such a confrontation?

The first step is to visualize *savage* scenarios. For example: Two or more suicidal killers wielding box cutters stand between you and the cockpit door—two psychopaths standing between you and you ever seeing your loved ones again, between you and the rest of your life!

A terrifying scene? Yes. A real-life combat scenario requiring a more intense degree of both *focus* and *ferocity* than if you were training for a refereed sporting event.

With all due respect to the many fine professional fighters who train 24–7 for kickboxing and even for no-holds-barred "Ultimate" and "Extreme" fights, the type of focus and ferocity needed to survive DTS kill-or-be-killed combat is quite different, no matter if that life-or-death struggle is played out in a back alley in Atlanta or a cramped cave in Afghanistan.

FOCUS

We live in especially troubling times. Steel yourself to do what must be done. However beautiful your particular martial art, never forget the "martial" part. Train with realism. Create realistic combat scenarios in your mind, the more *violent* and *terrifying* those

7. Ninja "monk."

Looks can be deceiving.

A. *Hat.* Large hat can conceal many weapons. Hat(s) can also be used as weapons themselves, their edges augmented with hidden razors. Larger hats can be used as shields to obscure a foe's vision and as a protective covering when facing a foe armed with a bladed weapon.

B. *Fan*. Ninja often augmented innocent-looking fans with razors. Heavier fans could also be made out of metal. Larger fans could be used to obscure a foe's line of sight.

C. *Ornaments* (earrings, pins, rings, etc.) can be used to startle an opponent (when thrown), to cut a foe (see illustrations 83 and 84) and even to strangle (e.g., "prayer beads" reinforced with strangling wire, etc.).

D. *Clothing*. Any type of clothing can be useful, from reversible clothing that allows you to instantly disguise yourself, to voluminous robes that allow you to distort your silhouette at night, to clothing with hidden pockets and with weapons sewn into them.

E. *Voluminous robe(s)* and other loose clothing allow you to hide weapons and so on inside.

F. *Sash*. The sash worn around the waist could be used like any rope: to strangle, to facilitate climbing, to bind wounds, and to set booby traps. Belts are the modern-day equivalent. Also, some clothing can be torn into thin strips and used for the same purposes.

G. *Cloaks*. Medieval Ninja often sported cloaks (made of cloth, straw, even feathers) designed to help distort their outline and/or used to "blind" a foe. The original "cloak" and dagger!

H. *Footwear* could be augmented with any manner of spikes to augment kicking and/or climbing. Ninja wore various types of special footwear, designed to fit climate (e.g., snowshoes), including footwear designed to fool pursuers into thinking the Ninja was going in the opposite direction.

I. *Walking staffs* were mandatory traveling tools (see illustration 77).

images the better. "The harder the whetstone, the sharper the knife" (Lung, 2003:133).

In all your training within the Nine Halls, your focus—your intent—must be to learn the lesson and/or *do the job right the first time,* with a minimum of excess effort and distraction.

When we apply this principle to combat training, our ideal becomes to defeat our foe with one focused strike. In Japanese, this intent is called *"Ikken Hisatsu!"* (lit. "to kill with one blow").

It doesn't matter if your weapon of choice is a ridge hand to the throat or a 12-gauge slug through his chest, the goal is always the same: the total defeat of your enemy. When it's a life-or-death struggle—your life versus his death!—your focus and intent must always be to finish your enemy before he finishes you.

Thus "focus," as spoken of in Ninja Nine Halls training, consists of two parts:

First, using focus to help us visualize (i.e., "see" in our "mind's eye") how we should—and will!—react to a particular DTS when it appears.

Second, "focus" refers to our developing the ability to "block out" all extraneous distractions to concentrate 100 percent on our immediate goal—whether that immediate goal is our striking down an enemy or preventing that enemy from striking us down.

Thus, when training, whether doing *kata* practice forms, punishing the heavy bag, or free sparring, we must always visualize the fiercest of foes, even when training alone. This doesn't mean we intentionally hurt our training partners, it simply means we visualize ourselves delivering the telling blow each time we strike our foe.

Our intent must be that, "If I only get *one* shot, I'm gonna make that shot count," no matter that in actual combat we may succeed in striking our enemy with several blows—*put the focus and ferocity into each blow as if it is the only hit you will get!*

The *Hagakure,* the "bible" of the Samurai, teaches that a warrior should meditate (i.e., imagine) himself dying by any and all horrible manners—for example, being cut down in battle, falling from a cliff—all to better prepare himself for when the Old Gray Mower actually comes calling.

Recent scientific research has confirmed what *yogis* and other Masters of the East have known for centuries: that visualizing something in the mind triggers the same body responses as actually doing the actual activity. That's why Olympic-level atheletes all use visualization.

Only *focus* can defeat *fear.*

It sometimes helps to see "fear" as an acronym for "False Evidence Appearing Real," since so many of our fears are merely products of our runaway imagination. These kinds of fears quickly dissipate when we focus on the job at hand and stop "awful-izing" about what *might* happen.

Here then is the Ninja's secret for overcoming fear: *Fear never arrives!* In other words, we fear what will happen *when*—in the future—a DTS arises, when—in the future, whether an hour from now or in the next minute—our enemy attacks, when he actually strikes at us.

Once this actually happens, there is no time for fear, only time to react (hopefully, as we have correctly trained ourselves to correctly react).

Therefore, fear is always in the future, it never really arrives. It is always a day, an hour, or even a minute away. Therefore, fear isn't real in the here and now.

This doesn't mean there aren't real dangers stalking us, dangers we should prepare against.

But whereas the dangers might be real . . . the *fear* is not.

Fear never arrives.

———

The "ideal" is to (1) *always be prepared* (2) *for anything* that might happen in (3) *any situation.*

This is an impossible goal. Shit happens.

However, dedicating ourselves to training correctly and realistically, when the time comes, our mind and body just *might* take care of us.

On September 11, 2001, some of those trapped on those doomed planes had an opportunity to fight back—and did!

Others, caught up in that fateful day—those busy going about their daily routine inside the Twin Towers, unaware of the tragedy unfolding—literally never saw it coming.

Yet even in a situation seemingly beyond our control, such as finding ourselves trapped in a burning skyscraper, the better overall condition we're in—physically and mentally—the better our chances of survival are—if only because we can mentally swallow our urge to panic long enough to will our shaking legs to run down a flight of stairs and/or jump out of the way of falling debris.

When training, *visualize* yourself in the worse-case scenario, whether physical one-on-one combat or a natural disaster. The more realism we inject into our training, the closer we raise our "stress" level to approximate that of an actual DTS, the better our chances of survival when/if a real threat of similar caliber materializes.

We've already established that we can't possibly anticipate every possible situation, but we can use our imagination to practice for as many variations as possible.

This is one reason that *only a small fraction of your "Ninja" training takes place in the dojo.*

Miyamoto Musashi said, "Your everyday stance should be the same as your combat stance."

Standing in line at the local supermarket, you should still be in your "combat stance," that is, alert, aware of your surroundings, not standing with your head down reading the headlines on the *National Enquirer.*

Instead, spend the time increasing your powers of observation and concentration.

For example: Why does that hooded punk standing in the checkout line in front of you keep his hands in his pocket? Is he just playing pocket pool or fingering a firearm? Why does he keep shifting nervously from foot to foot? Why does he keep glancing out the front window? Could he be looking to see if his getaway ride is still there?

Shazam! Suddenly you're a hostage in a botched robbery and at the mercy of a couple of crackheads!

While waiting for a taxi or preparing to board a bus or commercial airliner, imagine the worse-case scenario that might require you to choose "flight or fight."

When it comes to your survival and the survival of your loved ones, *become a pessimist*. Make "September Eleventh" your training mantra.

Form realistic images in your mind when training—the more terrifying the better. And don't make the mistake of imagining yourself doing some fantastic martial arts flying kick, knocking out the bad guy and getting a medal from the mayor. Instead, just see yourself doing "whatever it takes" to survive. *Masakatsu!*

Create fierce training scenarios that *involve your whole body and mind*.

Knowledgeable Martial arts instructors watch, not just how a student's right hand strikes forward, but how the student's left hand hangs limp (something that never happens when you visualize 100 percent). In other words, in a real fight, you never lower your guard, even for a second.

Likewise, don't be dazzled by how an opponent throws a kick, instead note whether he "lands with a hand," in a combat stance, ready to continue the fight if need be.

FEROCITY

"Once the threat is upon us, once the wolves are at the door and the beast is at our throat, there is no time to fear, only time to react" (Skinner, 1995:10).

When a medieval Ninja was sent on a stealth mission to infiltrate an enemy castle, he (or she) had to stay focused, never knowing when he might turn a corner to find himself confronted by an enemy sentry a scant few feet away.

When this happened, the Ninja had to instantly "bridge the gap," crossing the distance between himself and his enemy, to unleash a no-nonsense devastating attack before the sentry could pull a sword and/or sound an alarm.

Nowadays, this scenario is still the same, no matter if it's you having to "bridge the gap" before your stealth mission is discovered, or your having to instantly defend yourself from a fanatical terrorist attacking you—a terrorist who's been trained to "bridge the gap" himself!

"Ferocity" refers to (1) your ability to instantly "release/trigger" your attack and (2) striking into the enemy with *overwhelming force*.

In the next section on the *Silent Shout,* we discuss techniques for instantly "releasing" the Ninja attack strategies and tactics you learn.

The second part of this equation, attacking/counterattacking with "overwhelming force," does not necessarily mean using only physical force. We can also "overwhelm" a foe using psychological ploys such as misinformation.

Sun Tzu said that "If my enemy doesn't know where I intend to attack, he must prepare everywhere; having to prepare everywhere, he will be strong nowhere."

Thus, we can "overwhelm" an enemy with too much (mis)information, confusing him. This is not all that different from overwhelming an enemy with a flash and flourish of fierce fist and foot strikes.

The key to ferocity is to focus our attack (whether physical or psychological) and then continue that attack unrelentingly.

In physical combat, this unrelenting attack strategy manifests as the "Collapsing Principle" (see the First Hall—Unarmed Combat).

In mental terms, this means "overloading" an enemy's defenses, either by bombarding him with true information on just how helpless his position is and/or by feeding him false "intel" (misinformation and propaganda) designed to overwhelm his fighting spirit.

Thus, through focus and ferocity we can correctly decipher our enemy's intentions beforehand and then overwhelm him with a ferocious attack designed to destroy his aggression—ideally before it is ever fully formed in his fevered feral mind.

In other words, Ninja overwhelm their foes by striking first and striking hard with explosive speed and power.

But how are we to acquire such explosive speed and power, you ask?

Good question.

Good learning begins with good questions.

Developing Explosive Speed and Power

Mastering any martial art technique begins and ends with correct practice.

Note we said *correct* practice.

Despite the old adage, "Practice" *does not* "make perfect," not if we are taught a movement *incorrectly* in the first place, in other words, by not being shown—and held to—the *correct form*.

Learning *correct form* is like digging an irrigation ditch. The deeper we dig that ditch, the more certain we can be that our ditch will serve its purpose when the time comes, that once we loose the flood waters, unimpeded, the water will rush down the deep and straight ditch, *picking up speed* as it goes. Should anything—or *any-one!*—have the misfortune to get in the way of this speeding wall of water, they will be crushed by the power of the forceful torrent!

In this same way, as Ninja students we must train both our mind and muscles to flow unimpeded along the correct pathways of response and action. Then, when a DTS confronts us, "instinctively" we will respond instantly, appropriately, and effectively.

THE NINJA SECRET OF SPEED

Ever accidentally scald your hand under a hot water faucet? Remember how you snatched your hand out from under that scalding water *before* you even had time to feel the pain?

Even without training, the muscles in your arm pulled your hand to "safety" *before your brain even had time to realize, register, and respond to the pain signal!*

But how is it possible for you to move so fast . . . actually *faster than thought?*

Here's how it works: Sensors in your scalded hand instantly flash signals to your brain and then "wait" for your brain to identify the problem and send "pain" signals back to the hand. While this communication only takes a micro-second to accomplish, that's still too slow because, on its way to the brain, that signal must first pass through your spinal cord (which controls your physical functions). And as soon as the pain signal reaches the spinal cord, your spinal cord sends an immediate reflex signal back, making your hand jerk out from under the scalding water.

Most important, this is done *without the conscious command* of the brain.

Here then is your *proof* that *you can move faster than pain!*

This is exactly the kind of "instinctive reflex" the Ninja warrior cultivates.

As we will soon see when studying in the First Hall—Unarmed Combat, Ninja crafted both their defensive/offensive strikes and counterstrikes from *natural reactions,* for example, instinctively throwing up our hands to protect ourselves when attacked (see also the Fifth Hall, Specialized Combat Training).

Through repeated practice we train our bodies to react even while our brains are still processing incoming data.

Respect your bestial birthright. We were petty prey struggling to survive an unforgiving world long before we evolved brains big enough and ruthless enough to elevate us to the rank of Prime Predator.

Ninja Rule: Make friends with your body and it will take care of you.

In a kill-or-be-killed DTS our "fight or flight" instinct kicks in and we either beat feet ("flight"—always a respected option for guerilla fighters and Ninja!) or else we instinctively strike out ("fight") to beat the hell out of our enemy.

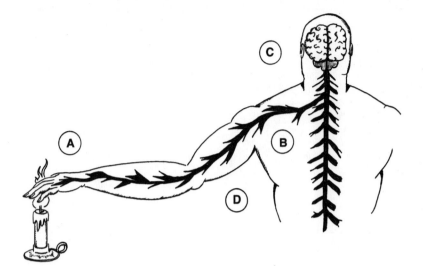

8. "Faster than pain!"

A. As your hand encounters "pain," messages race along the nerves in your arm, toward your brain.
B. The nerve impulses from the arm must pass "through" the spinal cord on their way to the brain.
C. Before the brain has time to process and send a "pain" signal back to the burning hand . . .
D. The spinal cord has already sent a message to the muscles of the arm to jerk the hand away from the flame; pulling the hand away from the "pain" before pain is actually felt—thus, your muscles can move faster than pain!

Seeing as how this "flight or fight" response is inborn in us, why not "build on" these *natural reactions,* honing survival instincts we all already possess into even more effective tactics for survival?

That's exactly what Ninja do!

The best martial arts techniques are always extrapolations of *natural reactions,* for example, the natural reaction of throwing up our arms to block an overhead attack is easily "reprogrammed" into an effective "X-Block."

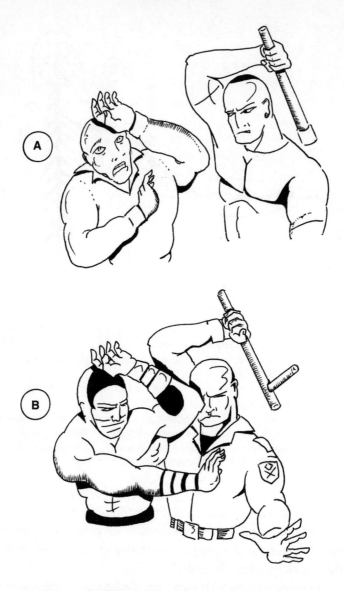

9. "Natural Reactions," such as

A. Instinctively throwing up your arms in response to an overhead attack . . .

B. Can easily be turned into a viable defensive-offensive technique.

In turn, successfully X-Blocking an attack positions us for an effective counterstrike.

Likewise, the natural reaction of catching an apple thrown toward our face is nearly identical to the arm and hand movements Ninja use when blocking a punch to the face and countering with a "Tiger's Claw" counterstrike.

Thus, the key to adding speed to our martial arts technique is to "program" reactions into our muscles (and mind) designed to be triggered automatically when we are threatened—reactions based on *natural responses* we already possess.

THE SILENT SHOUT

In an offensive situation, we must train ourselves to "release" our body to do what it does naturally as well as what it has been trained to do. This is called "bridging the gap," that is, closing the distance between you and your enemy and striking him down before he has a chance to attack you or to defend against your attack.

Too often in a DTS, the untrained body "freezes." Whereas fleeing from a superior force is often just common sense—and acceptable strategy—to stand paralyzed, like a deer trapped in headlights, is to invite death.

Thus, all knowledgeable martial arts instructors teach students how to trigger (i.e., "release") their innate and trained combat responses. Karate students are taught to scream out a "Kiai!" (Jp. "Spirit Shout") when striking, not only to "terrorize" their enemy (i.e., make *him* freeze) but also because bellowing like a banshee "startles" us free from paralysis. This, in turn, "releases" the trained body to do what it has to do to survive.

Since Ninja activities often require stealth, wailing out a blood-curdling war cry is not always an option, so Ninja students are taught to use a *Kiai-kime,* a "silent shout" when attacking. Kime-kiai is a literal and figurative "tightening and focus" (kime) of both mind and body that is then released (like a shout) on the enemy.

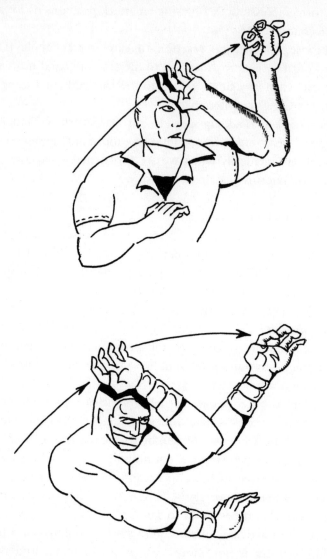

10. "Natural Reactions" such as catching a softball tossed to us, can easily be turned into the "natural" reaction of a Jonin-Overhead Block followed by a Descending Tiger's Claw attack to a foe's upper body.

FORM + SPEED = POWER!

Before stepping foot inside the Nine Halls, those new to the Ninja realm must memorize and internalize this mantra:

"Form plus Speed equals Power!"

Consider: A bullet tossed from your hand will bounce off an attacker's chest. Yet that same bullet exploding from the barrel of a pistol easily penetrates that same attacker's chest, slamming into him with enough power to get the job done.

What has changed in this equation?

What's changed is that *form* (the rifling in the barrel causing the bullet to spin and thus fly straighter), combined with the *speed* at which the slug explodes from the pistol, adds up to more impact, that is, *power!*

Thus: Form plus Speed equals Power.

This same formula can—must!—be applied to all Ninja techniques.

Don't make the mistake of assuming that this "Form + Speed = Power" applies only to the *physical* aspects of Ninja training.

Indeed, this same formula can be applied literally and figuratively to all aspects of Ninja training, to all aspects of the Nine Halls of Training.

In other words, in whatever task we undertake to learn (e.g., the Sixth Hall—The Art of Disguise), we first dedicate ourselves to learning the proper form (in this case, learning the various types of disguise tools and ploys available). We then slowly hone our performance of those movements intricate to proper and speedy performance of those forms (e.g., learning to quickly slip into various disguises).

Having accomplished these two preliminary tasks and having paired proper form with speed, we can now add the *power* of this newly acquired skill to our options, increasing our opportunities for victory.

"In seeking, know. In knowing, strike! In striking, strike well! And in striking well, accomplish all things!"
—Wan Tzu

III. THE NINE HALLS

RIN,
"The Power Fist,"

grants the seeker the attribute of *strength* and

opens the way to entrance into

THE FIRST HALL:
UNARMED COMBAT

INTRODUCTION: "T^3"

THE NINJA WATCHWORD FOR MASTERING THE FIRST HALL: Unarmed Combat is "Masakatsu," literally "By any means necessary, what ever works" to get the job done.

In fact, "Masakatsu," which is a combination of mantra and war cry, is the underlying attitude we must embrace for *all* our Ninja training.

While many "traditionalist" martial arts instructors dutifully, unquestioningly, pass along the same—unchanged—techniques that were in turn passed down to them through "Masters" lineages—some respectable, some dubious—the only "tradition" Ninja warriors have is *a tradition of breaking tradition!*

Survival is more important than servitude to tradition.

The Ninja does not limit himself (or herself) to one style or school of unarmed martial arts. Instead of "idealizing" a particular style of fighting, the Ninja freely "steals" from any and all martial arts, quickly discarding any superfluous "tradition" and "posturing" in favor of the most effective combat technique.

Taking into consideration their own advantages and disadvantages of birth (i.e., height, weight, body mass, etc.), Ninja students first learn "the basics," with an especial eye toward spotting the similarities shared by *all* martial arts.

To better systemize and accelerate their mastery of unarmed combat, Ninja divide their understanding and training into three distinct yet overlapping phases: *tools, techniques,* and *targeting.*

Tools are the natural "weapons" we're born with: hands, feet, elbows, knees, teeth, and other parts of the body we can use to block an attack and/or strike back into an attacker.

Techniques are the many ways (e.g., directions of attack, methods of moving, etc.) we use these natural tools either defensively and/or offensively—often one and the same objective.

Targeting refers to our reaching a level of martial mastery where we can effectively wield our natural tools and techniques to protect ourselves and loved ones.

Tools

The number-one Ninja *Taijutsu* "Unarmed Combat" Rule: *Every part of your body can be used as a weapon!* Not surprising, the unarmed fighting "tools" are many.

For a Ninja, *unarmed combat is what you do "in between" one weapon and another.* In other words, your unarmed combat training serves you best when you are prevented from getting to and using your other weapons. This is why the fighting "tools" of Ninja unarmed combat closely mirror those actual weapons we will learn to use in subsequent Halls—wooden weapons, bladed weapons, and Flex-Ten weapons.

Caught without a knife, a Ninja's slashing hands and stabbing fingers become his sword and dagger.

Trapped without a *bo* fighting-staff (see illustration 7), a Ninja's legs became his fighting staff to stab into his foe and/or sweep his foe's legs out from under him.

Likewise, the "Methods of Movement" and techniques we will later need for mastering traditional weapons like *jo* short fighting sticks and bladed weapons are similar to (or the same) as movements we've already "programmed" into our mind and muscle via the study—*and sweat!*—invested in the First Hall of Unarmed Combat.

BLOCKING TOOLS

Anything you can use to strike into a foe, you can also use to block that foe's attack—hands, arms, legs, knees, and feet.

However, the first Ninja rule of blocking is *never block . . . strike!*

Rather than first blocking and then counterstriking into a foe, Ninja fighters *strike into the offending limb,* using the initial forceful "blocking" movement to cripple the attacking limb.

Recall that Ninja students learn to strike each blow as if it is the only blow they will be able to land: *Ikken hisatsu!* ("Kill with one blow!"). This is similar to the Samurai archer's motto: "One arrow, one death!" and identical to the sniper's mantra: "One bullet . . . one less problem!"

Thus, every "block" the Ninja unleashes is intended to disable (stun or break) the attacker's offending limb.

This is accomplished by using our two old friends: *focus* and *ferocity*.

"Soft" Blocks. Even when a Ninja's "block" appears to be "soft" (i.e., intended to deflect a blow rather than disable it), that block is still used to "springboard" into a forceful counterstrike.

Therefore, whether being used as a counterstrike itself, or as a "springboard" from which to launch a telling counterstrike, Taijutsu "blocks" are always viewed as strikes.

For example, a "Palm-Up Block" doubles as a "Monkey-Paw Strike."

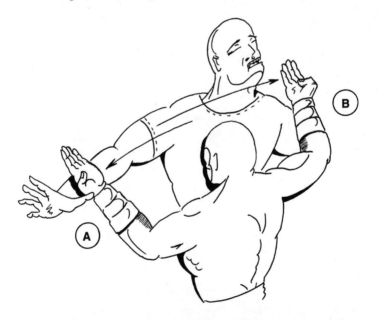

11. The Palm-Up Block, used to block an attacking arm outward (A) uses the same movement used for an effective "Monkey's Paw" strike across the throat of an attacker (B).

Your blocking hand gathers additional energy for a counterstrike when it uses the attacker's blocked arm as a springboard.

For example, use the "bounce" stolen from your foe's blocked arm as a spring board to launch a "Tiger's Claw Strike" into his face and throat.

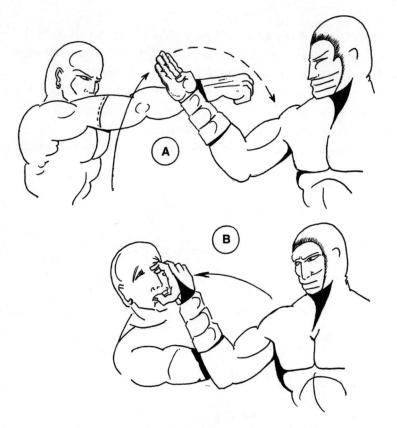

12. "Springboarding"

A. Bouncing his Palm-Up Block off his attacker's arm . . .
B. The Ninja uses his foe's blocked arm like a springboard, adding more force and momentum to his follow-up "Tiger's Claw" attack by "rebounding" his own striking arm forward.

This same springboarding principle is used in kicking.

For example, having stifled a foe's forward advance by striking into his leading knee with a "Chinese Cross Kick," instead of placing your kicking leg down, allow it to "ricochet" off his lead leg and reroute your kicking leg into a "Side-Thrust Kick."

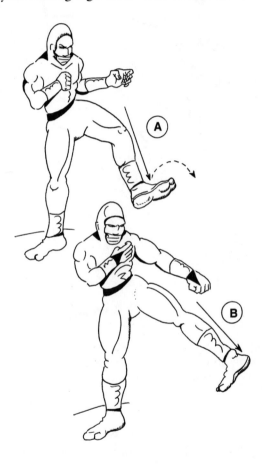

13. "Rebounding with foot strikes"

A. Striking into your opponent with a "Chinese-Cross Kick," the instant your kick connects with your opponent's leg . . .

B. "Rebound" off the leg, using the force of the impact to "springboard" your leg into your follow-up "Side-Thrust Kick."

14. The Waist Rule:
"If it's below your waist, block it with your legs. If it's above your waist, block it with your hands."

Three Blocking Rules. Blocking Rule #1: There are *no blocks.*

Blocking Rule #2: If it's below your waist, "block" it with your legs. Above the waist, "block" it with your hands.

In other words, block low-level kicking attacks and/or punches to your lower abdomen by raising your knees and legs.

Higher-level attacks targeting your chest and head are blocked with your hands.

Blocking Rule #3: Build all your "blocks" on *natural reactions.*
Remember: The best martial arts techniques are built on just
such *natural reactions.* Review the section on *Developing Explosive
Speed and Power.*

STRIKING TOOLS (DAIKENTAIJUTSU)

Faced with a Dire-Threat Situation (DTS), Ninja immediately
assess their options for attacking/counterattacking using three suc-
cessive options or perimeters: (1) using *weapons* (either traditional
weapons or "environmental weapons" that are gleaned from your
immediate surroundings), (2) striking into the foe with kicks and
punches, and (3) grappling a foe to the ground.

Having successfully positioned yourself "out of the line of fire,"
you then strike back into your foe, ideally with a single finishing
strike—Ikken hisatsu!

Anything on your body (or *in* your hand for that matter) can be
used to strike into and disable your opponent.

Every DTS is different. You must always be ready to adapt to
flux and circumstance. Thus, a Ninja's response (e.g., a kicking response versus a punching response, versus a grappling counter) is
influenced by both his own position and the position of his foe.

Your options of response and striking tools so far as to *where*
and *how* to strike into your foe will be determined to a great extent
by how and where (distance from you) your foe is standing.

Your chances of winning are limited only by your imagination . . . and *desperation!* Focus and ferocity.

All your striking tools can be used to strike any number of targets on your opponent's body.

Ninja Taijutsu striking tools include hands, feet, and "secondary"
weapons such as elbows, knees, and head butts.

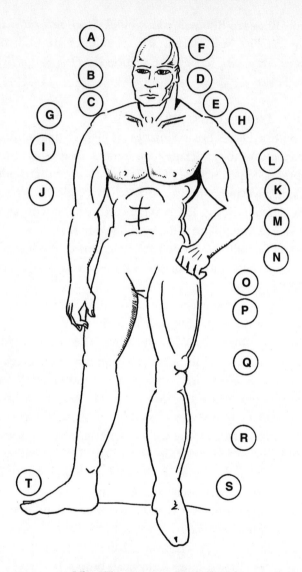

15a. "Targets on a Foe's Body"

A. Head: Kill the head and the body dies.
B. Eyes: Any attack to the eyes will startle your foe, eliciting a "flinch reaction" you can take advantage of. Striking into the eyes (see illustration 19) can temporarily and permanently blind

a foe. A foe can also be blinded by liquids, powders, and smokes targeting the eyes.

C. Nose: Any forceful blow to the nose can disorient an attacker. Can't breathe, can't fight; thus any attack that interferes with a foe's breathing (strikes, powders, toxic fumes, etc.) works to your advantage.

D. Ears: Any sharp blow to the ears (e.g., open hand "Palm Strikes") can damage the eardrums, disorienting, rendering unconscious, and even killing a foe. Any dirk or icepick-like weapon (including writing pens, pencils, knitting needles, etc.) jammed into the brain via the ear will cause instant death. Any loud noise (e.g., firecrackers, "Flash-Bang" grenades) can be used to startle a foe, providing an opening you can exploit to attack and/or escape (see illustration 23).

E. Mouth: Broken teeth can choke a foe. Any toxic substance attacking the mouth can interfere with a foe's ability to breathe.

F. Temple: A strike to the temple can cause pain, unconsciousness, and even death (see illustrations 18, 20, 27, 31, 33, 67, 68, 71, 73, 75 and 85).

G. Throat: Strikes and/or strangling attacks to the throat, specifically restricting and/or crushing the larynx (voice box), can incapacitate and/or kill a foe (see illustrations 11, 20, 32, 33, 41, 49, 50, and 51).

H. Neck: Anywhere along the sides or back of the neck can be attacked with solid blows to produce pain, unconsciousness, and even death (see illustrations 19, 37, and 47–50).

I. Clavicles: Attack the "collarbones" with downward "Hammerfist" and Shuto "Karate chops" designed to shatter these bones. Note: A broken collarbone can be forced down to penetrate the subclavicle arteries running just under the collarbones. Severing these arteries can cause unconsciousness in seconds and death within minutes (see illustrations 18 and 19).

J. Solar Plexus: Any forceful hand, foot, or weapons strike to the solar plexus can knock the breath out of an opponent, resulting in his disorientation and/or unconsciousness (see illustrations 26 and 73).

K. Ribs: See illustrations 21 and 29.

L. Armpits: An often-neglected target. Striking up into the armpit with a sharp object, or with a nukite "Spearhand" Strike can incapacitate the entire arm. Likewise, forceful "Tiger's Claw" grips into the armpit, at the juncture of the pit and "the pecs," can also interfere with an arm's mobility (see illustration 29).

M. Elbow: Striking into the elbow, breaking it, or otherwise "locking out" the elbow can effectively destroy a foe's arm, destroying much of his ability to continue a fight (see illustrations 40, 41, and 46).

N. Wrists: Any sharp blow can stun and/or incapacitate the wrist. The wrist is also susceptible to wrenching twists and Aikido-esque locks (see illustration 45).

O. Hands: Fingers can be broken by both armed (bludgeon) and unarmed blows (Hammerfist). Fingers can also be wrenched and twisted to facilitate takedowns.

P. Groin: Targeted by both armed and unarmed blows (see illustration 68). The groin can also be seized and twisted during grappling.

Q. Knees: Foot strikes can shatter the knee (see illustrations 13 and 53). Strikes with the palm/hand can be used to "lock-out" the knee during grappling (see illustration 44).

R. Shins: Kicks to the shin can cause pain. Breaking the shin can incapacitate an opponent.

S. Ankles: Ankles damaged by kicks and sweeps can incapacitate a foe. Ankles can also be "locked-out" using a technique similar to Wrist-locks (see illustration 45).

T. Feet: Feet damaged by bone-crushing stomps and/or by weapons blows will impair a foe's mobility.

15b. "Targets from Behind"

A. Ears

B. Base of Skull: Any forceful blow to the juncture where the skull and spinal column meet ("Atlas & Axis") can cause pain, disorientation, unconsciousness, and death. "Breaking the neck" at this juncture, either through blows or due to wrenching, will paralyze the body and result in death unless the victim is treated immediately (see illustrations 37, 48, 49, 75, and 76). This is also a prime knife target when attacking a sentry.

C. Seventh Vertebrae: Any solid strike into this target can stun an opponent. This is also a prime target for a "sentry-removal" knife attack.

D. Spine: Solid blows anywhere up and down the "backbone" can cause pain and possible paralysis. Severing (or otherwise acutely damaging) the spine anywhere along its length will result in paralysis to the body below that point.

E. Kidneys: Any sharp blow up into the kidney will result in intense pain, internal damage, and possible death. The kidneys are also prime targets for sentry-removal knife attacks.

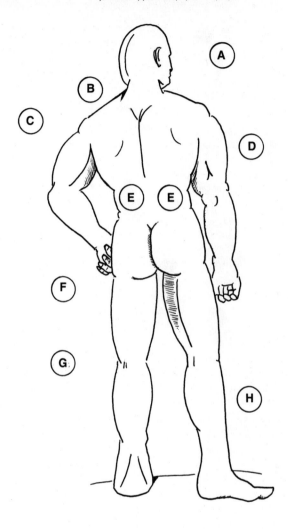

F. Groin: Kicks and Knife-hand strikes up into the groin from
behind can be used to unbalance and incapacitate a sentry.

G. Knees: A solid stomp to the back of the leg will unbalance an
opponent. A painful Tiger's Claw attack to the tendons at the
back of the knee can also unbalance and/or interfere with a
foe's mobility.

H. Lower Leg: Striking/sweeping into the calf and/or ankle can
unbalance an opponent (see illustrations 29, 32, 34, 38, 43, 44,
47, 48, 53, and 76).

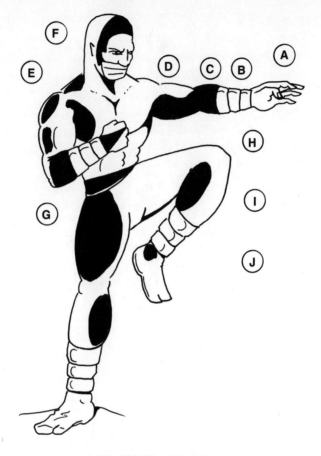

16. "Striking Tools"

A. Hands: See illustrations 11, 12, 17–24, 29, 30, 41–46, 48, 50, 67–69, and 75.

B. Wrist (aka "Turtle's Head"): See illustration 31.

C. Forearm: See illustrations 32, 47–49, and 65.

D. Elbows: See illustrations 33, 37, and 39.

E. Shoulder: See illustration 34.

F. Head (includes biting with teeth and spitting, to distract): See illustration 35.

G. Hips: See illustration 36.

H. Knee: See illustration 37.

I. Shin: See illustrations 14 and 38.

J. Feet: See illustrations 13, 25–28, 38, 39, 52, 53, and 59.

Hand Striking Tools. Many martial arts schools, especially Chinese "Kung-fu" schools, use purposely distracting and confusing "animal" hand positions—Tiger, Crane, Praying Mantis, Snake, and so on.

Some of these hand postures serve as legitimate—and lethal!—striking tools. Some are used simply to identify a particular style and school. Still others are intended to intimidate the uninitiated.

Confronted by a foe flashing such arcane hand postures, don't get "psyched out."

Likewise, don't be intimidated by the prospect of having to master dozens of such hand positions and postures while training in the First Hall.

All these seemingly different and diverse hand positions are actually *only three:* the *Closed Hand,* the *Open Hand,* and the *Claw Hand.*

The Closed Hand can strike straight-in forward, upward ("uppercut"), and hooking-in, with a full hand like a Western boxer.

The Closed Hand can also strike as the two-knuckle horizontal "Karate" fist, or with the single-knuckle vertical "Chinese" Kung-fu style fist.

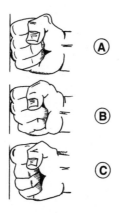

17. "The Three Fists"

A. Boxer's Fist (flat)
B. "Karate Fist" (first two knuckles)
C. "Chinese Fist" (single knuckle)

The Closed Hand also strikes downward like a "hammer" and can also be used as a "Back Fist."

18. "Closed Hand Attacks"

A. Backfist (strikes to temple)
B. Hammerfist (smashes collarbone)

The Open Hand can be used to both "stab" into an enemy like a knife *(nukite)* and to "chop" down like a sword *(shuto)*.

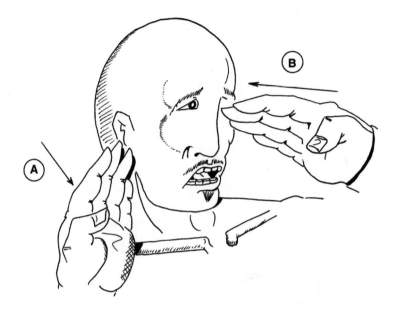

19. "Open Hand Attacks I"

A. "Shuto-swordhand" (chops into the side of the neck/smashes collarbone)

B. "Nukite-spearhand" (attacks eyes and throat). See also illustration 41.

The Open Hand can strike into "tighter" targets where the Closed Hand fist cannot, for example, into a foe's throat or up into his groin. These strikes are accomplished by inverting the Open Hand and striking with the "thumb forward" side. Karate calls this the *gyaku-shuto*, "Reverse Ridge-Hand." Kung-fu stylists call it the "Monkey's Paw."

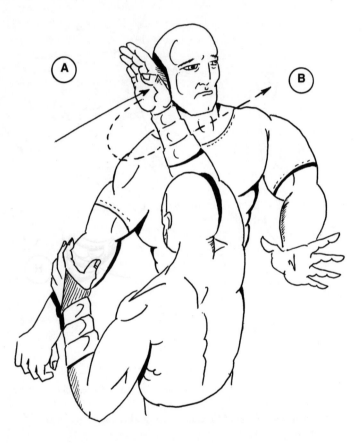

20. "Open Hand Attacks II"

A. "Monkey's Paw" (aka Inverted Swordhand) strikes to temple.
B. "Rebounding" off temple-strike, Monkey's Paw becomes Swordhand to slash across the throat.

The Open ("Sword") Hand can deliver more force into "hard" targets such as the ribs because its contact surface is smaller, therefore its power is not as distributed as a fatter fist. Also, in the case of ribs, the *shuto* can slash *in between* protective ribs.

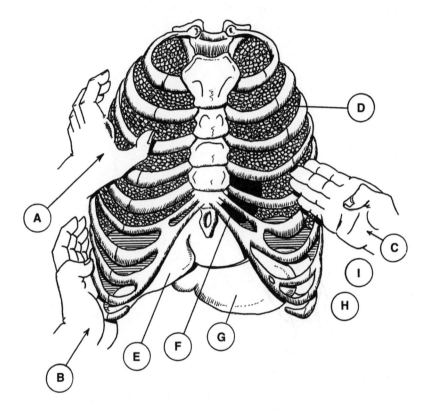

21. "Open Hand Strikes to Ribs"

A. "Tiger's Mouth" (between ribs)
B. "Palm Strike" (targeting "Floating ribs")
C. Nukite (between ribs)
D. Lungs
E. Liver
F. Heart
G. Stomach
H. Spleen
I. Diaphragm

The Claw Hand strikes and "tears" at targets.

Chinese Kung-fu has entire styles built around "Animal" clawing tools and techniques, for example, Dragon, Tiger, and Northern Eagle Claw styles.

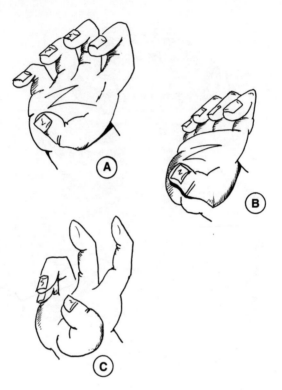

22. "Claw Hand Variations"

A. Tiger's Claw: Fingers fully splayed, variation of "Dragon's Hand": strike with palm-heel, follow through with a clawing attack that rakes across soft tissue (e.g., eyes, throat). See illustrations 23 and 24.

B. Dragon's Hand: Strike forward into your target, striking with the palm, immediately on impact, close the Dragon's Claw to seize a grip on foe's flesh.

C. Eagle's Claw: Clawing attack (directed against nerves and exposed "soft" muscle tissue). Thumb, Index, and Middle fingers splayed. Ring finger reinforces little finger.

Claw Hand ripping attacks target "soft" tissues—throat, eyes, testicles, and joint tendons—with painful strikes intended to instantly unbalance and/or cripple a foe.

Claw Hand strikes are often delivered from "oblique" striking angles that make it difficult if not impossible for a foe to block.

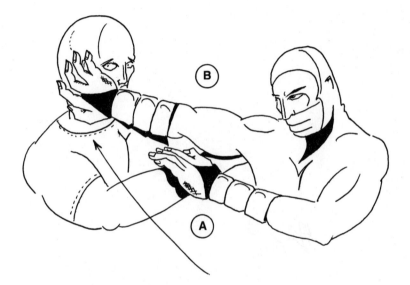

23. "Oblique Tiger's Claw Attack"

A. Having "smothered" foe's attacking arm with a Palm-down Block . . .
B. Strike "outward" and then inward with an Inverted Tiger's Claw strike, impacting first with the palm before then following through with a raking/ripping claw to foe's face and/or throat.

Claw Hand attacks are most effective when paired with initial "softening up" strikes. For example, a "Dragon-Claw Strike" involves first striking the target with a forceful "Palm Strike" that then "collapses" into a tearing Claw strike.

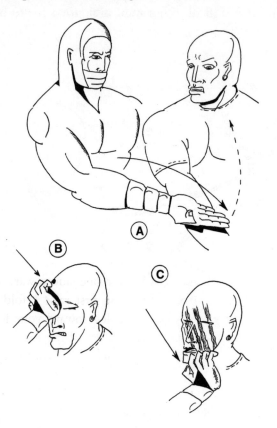

24. "Dragon's Hand Attack"

A. Using a Palm-up Block to turn aside your foe's attacking arm . . .

B. Rebound off your foe's blocked arm, coming over and down, striking down onto the bridge of his nose with the palm of your Dragon's Hand.

C. Following through with your Dragon's Hand, immediately on impact, close your striking hand into a clawing hand and rake it across/down your foe's face.

Kicking Tools. Kicks are our first striking weapon since a foe comes within striking range of our feet long before we can reach him with our fists.

Watch a good martial arts movie and you'll get the impression there are *hundreds* of different martial arts kicks. Not surprising, the prospect of having to master so many variations of kicks, let alone learning to defend against so many possible kicking attacks, is daunting to the beginner.

While it's true there are an endless variety of ways *to use* kicks, Ninja know there are actually *only four* types of kicks in all the martial arts. This is because anatomy and physics dictate that we can only extend our legs in one of four ways:

- **Front Kicks** strike forward vertically, first raising ("folding") your knee and then snapping or thrusting forward with the foot, striking with either the toe when wearing hard shoes or else with the ball of the foot or the heel when barefoot or when wearing soft-soled shoes.
- **Side Kicks** are executed with your one side toward the enemy. As with your front kicks, you first raise ("fold") your leading leg before thrusting your leg toward your foe on a horizontal plane—striking with the flat of the foot, the heel, or with the leading edge of the foot (aka "Swordfoot").
- **Round Kicks** circle up and around from the floor on a horizontal plane as you rotate our hips forward. There are two variations of Round Kicks: "Roundhouse" kicks that circle up and in, striking with the toe (when wearing hard shoes) or with the top of the foot or ball of the foot (when barefoot). The second variation is the "Hook Kick," which strikes first outward before "hooking" back in to strike with the heel.
- **Arching Kicks** (aka "Crescent Kicks" and "Axe Kicks") arc up and around vertically, an inverted "U," striking either outward (away from your "centerline") or inward (in toward your "centerline"), striking with the inside or outside edge of the foot.

25. "Front Kick Attacks"

A. Foot is lifted by contracting the knee vertically.
B. Foot is then either "snapped" or "thrust/pushed" forward
along a horizontal plane to strike with toe (when wearing stout
footwear), the pad of the foot (with toes bent back), or with the
heel of the foot (see also illustration 52).

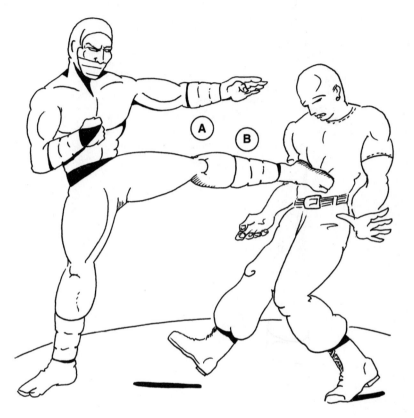

26. "Side Kick Attacks"

A. Foot is lifted by contracting the knee (see illustration 62).
B. "Chambered" foot then strikes forward along a horizontal plane, striking with either the sole, heel, or side ("swordfoot") of the foot (see also illustration 13 and 53).

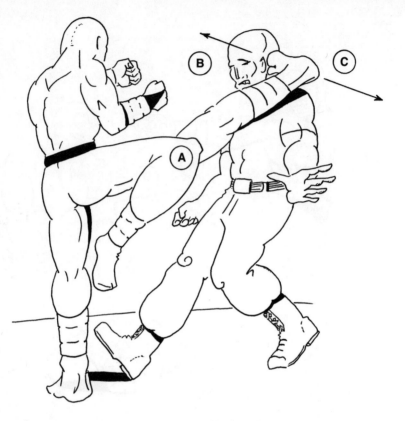

27. "Round Kick Attacks"

A. The attacking leg is lifted by contracting the knee vertically.

B. As the knee reaches its apex, suddenly rotate your hip forward as your knee turns onto a horizontal plane and your foot snaps out to strike with the toe (when wearing sturdy shoes) or with the pad of the foot, toes bent back (when barefoot).

C. The "Reverse Round Kick" (aka "Hook Kick") is performed identical to the Forward Round Kick (aka "Roundhouse") except that the Hook Kick reverses direction to strike with the heel as it slashes across its target.

Tip: The Hook Kick is especially effective when used to target an opponent's groin, for example, when you are both in a sides-facing position.

28. "Arcing Kick Attacks"

A. Contracting the knee upward.

B. Snap (do not "swing"!) your foot forward in an "arc" either outward from your body or inward to "slap" into your opponent.

C. This type of kick (aka "Crescent Kick") can also be used to disarm an attacker by sweeping his weapon away from your body and/or dislodging his weapon from his hand.

While there are only four kicks for the Ninja student to learn, the use of these four basic kicks is limited only by the Ninja's imagination and desperation.

For example, these four basic kicks easily become *dozens of kicks* once combined with *Methods of Movements* such as "Over-the-Fence" and with jumping, as favored by such schools as Korean Tae-Kwan-do and Okinawan Shotokan (see *Techniques* section below).

Two rules to remember when adding kicks to your *Daikentaijutsu* arsenal:

First: *Always land with a hand.* Follow-up your kick (whether you hit or miss your target) with a hand strike. Don't step back to admire your work. Use the speed and momentum of your "landing" (i.e., placing your kicking foot down), striking your already stunned foe with a finishing hand strike.

Correct hand striking *form* plus the *speed* and momentum of your "landing" equals additional *power* for your finishing strike.

Second rule: *Kick on the break.* When pushing away from a grappling attacker, kick as you separate. This is when a fighter is most likely to drop his guard. Professional kickboxers call this "kicking on the break." Formidable footboxers, for example, Thai kickboxers and French *Savate* fighters, are infamous for using this tactic.

When grappling, Ninja often employ the "Scorpion" kicking technique: Seizing hold of an opponent's arm(s) while simultaneously smashing into his legs and lower body with savage kicks—the way a scorpion first seizes its prey with its claws before striking with its deadly tail.

FYI: In his *Ping Fa,* Sun Tzu refers to a similar tactic that he calls the "Twice Striking Snake," that is, attack the serpent's head, and its tail strikes you. Grabbing for its tail, you are struck down by its deadly fangs.

29. "Land with a Hand"

A. Having thrown a "Left Front Snap Kick" . . .
B. Land in a low squat, striking your foe with a solid Left hand strike to his solar plexus/abdomen . . .
C. Shift left and follow your left hand strike with a right hand strike and/or collapsing-in elbow strike. (Note: This maneuver and series of strikes works well when you slip in and under a foe's hooking punch.)
D. Staying in close with your stunned opponent, immediately drop your left hand down behind his leg and, jerking his leg forward from the ankle, sweep him to the ground (see illustration 44).

Additional Striking Tools. Think beyond just striking with your hands and feet. Any hard—bony—part of your body can be used to strike your foe (see illustration 16).

As we will learn in the Fifth Hall: Specialized Combat Training, people suffer from "object fixedness," the shortcoming of seeing only one use for an object. This is especially true of Westerners, who all too often see the hand as only the boxer's closed fist.

However, the human hand is capable of so much more, of being used to create several additional weapons: "The Short-Fist" (aka "Leopard's Paw"), *Yubu* "Thumb-Fist," and the *Ippon-Ken* "Single-Knuckle Fist."

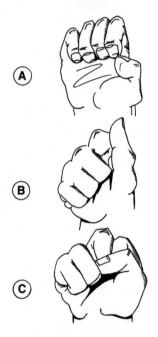

30. "Attacking Fist Variations"

A. "Leopard's Fist" (Striking with second knuckles joint).
B. "Yubu" ("Thumb Fist," striking with slightly extended thumb).
C. "Ippon-Ken" ("Single-Knuckle Fist," striking with slightly extended middle finger second knuckle).

Other additional striking weapons include:

♦ **Wrists** (aka "Turtle's Head"), used for both hard "blocking" and striking.

   In Chinese *Wu-shu*, striking with the wrist is a favored strike of Crane style Kung-fu, where it is called "Crane's Head."

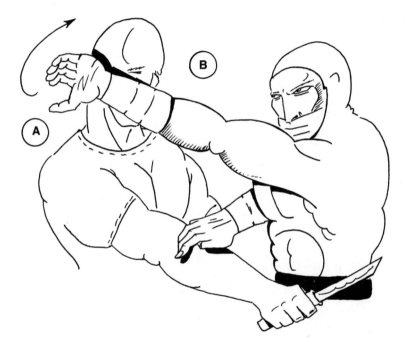

31. "Crane's Head Strike"

A. "Crane's Head" whip/snaps into foe's temple.
B. Follow through: Immediately on impact, "rebound" off foe's temple, whipping your attacking hand around to grab onto the back of his head (and/or neck) and force his head forward into your Horizontal Elbow Strike (see illustration 33).
Note: This head-grab move is similar to the Oblique Strike shown in illustration 23.

♦ **Forearms** can be used to both strike and strangle. Used to strike, the forearm can be used to "closeline" a foe (i.e., striking into his face with your extended forearm) and to strike up into a foe's throat and face.

The dreaded *Thuggee* highwaymen of India were masters of using their forearms as an offensive strangling weapon. Forearms can also be used to "lock-out" elbows and knees (see *Grappling Tools,* below).

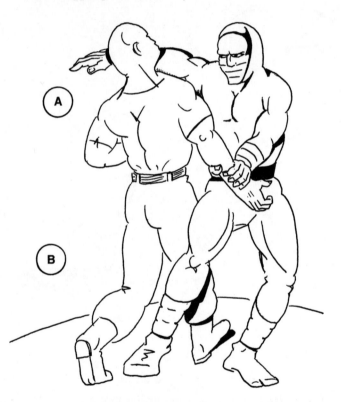

32. "Forearm Attack"

A. Employing the "Half-Moon Step" (see illustration 59) slip inside your opponent's defenses and slam your forearm into his upper torso, targeting his face and/or exposed throat.

B. Augment this Forearm Strike with an Outside Leg Reap.

♦ **Elbows,** also known as "Shortwing" strikes, are useful and forceful "close-in" striking tools. Drawback? Elbows require you to "close" with a foe.

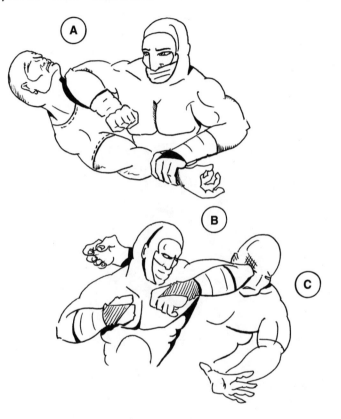

33. "Attacking with the Shortwing Elbows"

A. Strike forward either along a horizontal plane, or else with a Rising (vertical) Elbow strike targeting foe's temple, jaw, or throat (see also illustrations 9 and 44).

B. Strike backward along a horizontal and/or vertical line of attack when your foe is positioned behind or to the side of you (see illustration 65).

C. Employ a combination elbow attack, striking inward with a Forward Horizontal Strike before immediately reversing direction to strike with a Rearward Horizontal Elbow Strike (see Lung Prowant, 2000: 110–111).

♦ **Shoulder** strikes can unbalance and knock the breath out of an opponent by targeting his solar plexus.

Miyamoto Musashi's *A Book of Five Rings* teaches how a determined Samurai can strike an opponent hard enough with the shoulder to kill him.

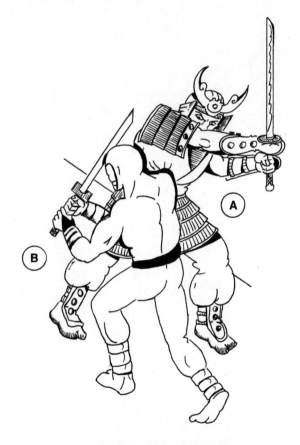

34. "Shoulder Striking"

A. Slipping in under your attacker's initial lunge, slam your shoulder into his ribs/abdomen, stopping his forward momentum/knocking the wind out of him.

B. From this advantageous position you are free to counterattack with a variety of moves targeting his midsection and lower body (see illustrations 29, 43, 44, 73, and 76).

♦ **Head butting** can stun and even kill. Head butts can be delivered forward, when locked in face-to-face combat, or backward, when seized from behind by a mugger.

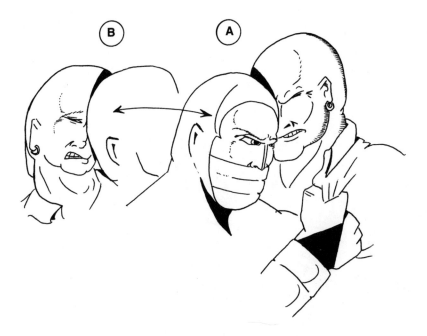

35. "Head Butt Attacks"

A. Strike forward, striking with the "ridge" on either side of your forehead.
B. Strike backward, into an attacker seizing you from behind.

FYI: The viability of headbutting is testified to by Okinawan *Karateka* breaking boards, heavy blocks of ice, and even bricks with their head.

In Eritrea-Ethiopia, an entire sport/martial art known as *Reisy* centers around vicious head-butt finishing moves (Prowant and Skinner, forthcoming).

♦ **Hips** are invaluable weapons in grappling-oriented arts such as *Juijutsu* and its sporting offshoot *Judo*.

Not only can a well-aimed hip strike a painful blow into your foe's side, hip, and groin, the resultant collision unbalances your foe, making him vulnerable to a takedown throw.

36. "Attacking with the Hips"

A. Having closed with your opponent, having seized a hold on his upper body, slam your hip into him, your hip slightly lower than his hip, "lifting" him with your hip as you . . .

B. Pull him around and down by turning/pulling his upper body.

C. As he hits the ground, follow through and finish with stomping technique.

◆ **Knees** are favored striking tools of all accomplished kick-boxers.

Knees can attack on a horizontal plane (like a "Round-house" kick) targeting the midsection, and in rising strikes targeting the groin and face (when a foe's head is pressed down into striking distance).

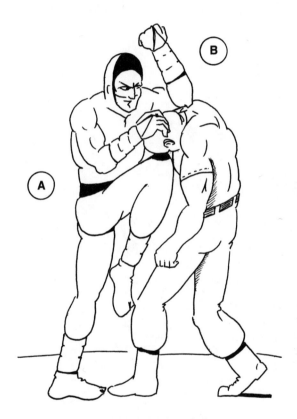

37. "Knee Attacks"

A. Strike into a foe's lower body (e.g., groin) with vertically Rising Knee Strikes and with Circling-in Knee Strikes (see illustration 62).

B. Strike into your foe's upper body (e.g., head) by forcing his head down into your Rising Knee Strike.

♦ **Shins** are striking tools usually reserved for professional kick-boxers who spend years "desensitizing" (and deforming) their shins by beating them against immovable objects.

However, with a minimum of training, the normal shin can be used to sweep-strike into the soft calf muscle at the back of a foe's leg, knocking him to the ground, where he can then be "finished off" with additional foot strikes (e.g., heel stomps, etc.).

38. "Attacking with the Shin"

A. Sweep in with the shin, striking the fleshy calf part of your opponent's lower leg, unbalancing him.

B. Immediately on striking with your shin, "hook" onto his leg with your foot and pull back and up, sweeping him to the ground. This is known as the "Returning Wave" kick-sweep.

These "Additional Striking Tools" can be used in concert with other hand and foot strikes and in concert with one another (see *The Collapsing Principle* in the section on *Targeting*).

"The more you know about how the human body is put together, the easier it is to take apart."

GRAPPLING TOOLS (JUTAIJUTSU)

A large percentage of unarmed combat encounters are decided by the application of a grappling technique: a chokehold, an "Arm-bar," or a wrist lock. Therefore, the dedicated and thorough martial artist wisely adds as much grappling science as he can to his arsenal.

To the novice, it first appears that grappling techniques require muscles to be used correctly. True, strength is always an asset when it comes to wrestling around with a foe; however, the best grappling techniques depend more on your mastery of movement and momentum than on muscle.

It also appears to the novice that there are an endless number of grappling options when in actuality there are a few basic methods of movement, holds, and "twist maneuvers" that, once mastered, allow us to add effective grappling to our Ninja arsenal.

Like all Ninja "Methods of Movement," Ninja grappling techniques (1) get us out of the line of fire while (2) simultaneously maneuvering us into an advantageous position from which to (3) restrict/control our enemy's further movement, while allowing us to (4) effectively counterattack with any and all tactics and techniques in the grappler's arsenal: painful joint attacks, bone-shattering breaks, and teeth-jarring takedowns!

Shift-Stifle-Seize-Subdue. Ninja grappling strategy can be summed up as: Shift-Stifle-Seize-Subdue.

Shift: Your foe has calculated where you will be standing when his punch, kick, or weapon hits you. Your job is *not* to be there when he gets there, to suddenly and surely shift out of the way an instant before his strike lands. This will cause him to overextend himself, to stumble, and to fall—*hard.*

Recall that martial arts, overall, is 90 percent positioning. Likewise, grappling is also 90 percent positioning. Therefore, Ninja employ "shifts," "pivoting," and a host of other "Methods of Movement," all designed to put them in the best possible *position* from which to figuratively and literally seize their foes by their throat and short hairs (see *The Three Shifts,* next section).

Stifle: Stifle your foe's forward momentum by "locking-out" his leading leg and/or breaking his leading-leg knee with a combination "Chinese Cross Kick" and/or low-level "Side Thrust Kick."

39. "Jamming"

Before a foe can fully initiate his attack . . .

A. "Smother" (i.e., jam) his attacking arm, ideally pinning his arm across his chest, preventing him from using either arm.

B. Jam his forward momentum and eliminate his ability to kick by kicking into his knee and/or lower leg (see illustration 13).

You can also stifle his forward momentum using "Roundhouse Kicks" to sweep out his leading leg (see *Lower Body Grappling*, below).

And by preventing him from retracting his attacking limbs.

Seizing: Having successfully stifled your foe's attacking momentum, you can then seize a hold on him.

Most commonly, we seize a hold on an attacker's extended limbs—arms or legs.

Remember that your attacker plans to strike you, retract his punching arm (or kicking leg), and then punch (or kick) again.

By seizing hold on his arm (or kicking leg), you not only prevent him from retracting and "reloading" his "guns," you also pull him off balance.

Seizing a hold on an opponent opens up new opportunities for counterattacking.

Don't limit yourself. You can use more than just your hands to trap an attacker. For example, we can likewise trap an attacker by "draping" our arm over his punching arm, catching it with our shoulder after "slipping" his punch.

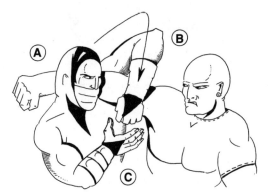

40. "The Drape-Over"

A. Having "slipped" inside your attacker's punching arm . . .
B. Circle your arm over his attacking arm, pinning his arm . . .
C. Immediately grab your draping arm with your opposite hand and suddenly squat, dropping your weight onto his arm, trapping/breaking his arm in an "Arm-Bar" (see illustration 46).

You can also seize-trap his arm by "Under-pinning."

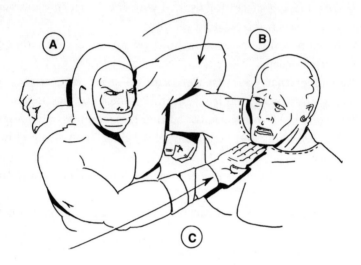

41. "The Eagle's Nest"

A. "Slipping" your attacker's punch . . .
B. Circle your arm up and over, pinning his attacking arm inside your arm pit (aka "The Eagle's Nest"). Apply pressure at the elbow.
C. Immediately counterattack with your free hand, elbow, knee, and so on.

Still another arm-trap technique blocks/redirects our attacker's punch into the crook of our elbow.

We can also seize hold of a foe's clothing and/or seize hold of his hair (see *Groundwork* and *Stangleholds,* below).

Subdue: Having trapped our foe's arm, we are then free to counterattack, for example, to *break his arm!*

To "subdue" an attacker means different things to different people. Some schools tell students to "become one" with their "poor

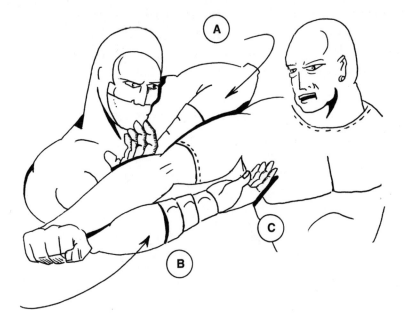

42. "Chinese Baseball"

A. As your attacker punches, shift your body outside his punch, while simultaneously performing a Cross-Body Palm-Block.

B. Use the force of your Cross-Body Palm-Block to "reroute" his punching arm into the crook of your opposite elbow. Immediately contract your arm, trapping his punching arm in the crook of your elbow, preventing him from retracting his punching arm.

C. His arm still trapped in the crook of your arm, counterattack with your free hand, and so on.

misguided" attacker and to "subdue" him with "a minimum of violence."

To Ninja, "subduing" a foe means you put him down and he doesn't get back up. Period.

Thus, Ninja grappling attacks can be divided into "Upper Body Grappling Attacks" and "Lower Body Grappling Attacks."

Lower-Body Grappling. Since our kicking legs give us further reach, our first option for bringing down a foe is to attack his legs, either kicking/breaking into his knee and/or shin (illustration 39), or else sweeping his legs out from under him.

43. "Cut the Corn"

A foe's legs can also be pulled out from under him using a variety of hand techniques:

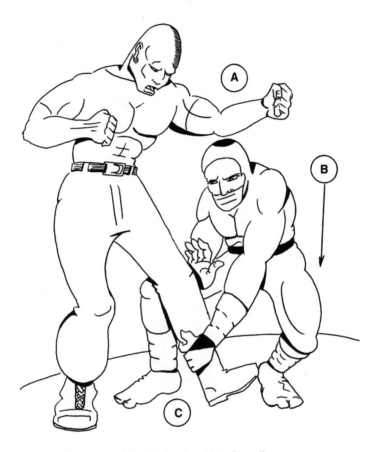

44. "Wolverine Takedown"

A. Slipping in under your foe's punching (or kicking) attack . . .
B. Attack into his leading/support leg's knee with a Palm-Strike (or Elbow Strike) while simultaneously pulling his leg, locking-out the leg, toppling him to the ground.
C. Finish with stomping technique.

Always finish a downed foe with stomps and kicks (see *Ground-working*, below).

Upper-Body Grappling. For those times when we cannot take an attacker's feet out from under him with kicks and sweeps, we must close and seize hold on him before applying a grappling finish.

There's a big difference between Eastern martial arts' strikes and punches (which often follow through by "collapsing" into the next technique), and the Western boxers' punches that jab and retract, jab and retract. The former lend themselves to trapping and seizing hold of a martial artist's "lingering" extended arm, whereas the Western boxer's hand quickly pulls back, making it much harder to seize hold of.

To compensate, Ninja aim a well-timed Elbow Strike (or any other forceful blows) directly into the attacking arm—stunning the attacking arm (or leg), preventing it from retracting, and giving the Ninja more time to seize the damaged (and dangling) limb.

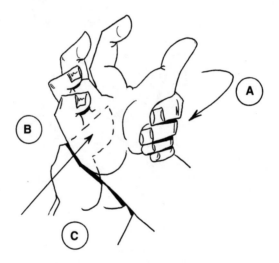

45. "Wrist Lock"

Seizing hold of your opponent's hand . . .
A. Your fingers press into the palm-pad of his hand while . . .
B. Simultaneously, your thumb jams into the back of his hand, cranking the hand inwards, towards the wrist.
C. Always augment "holds" and "locks" with strikes designed to "finish" the fight.

Grappling-oriented arts such as *jujutsu* and *aikido* teach dozens of joint-locking techniques. But joint locking basically comes down to two types: wrist and hand "twists" and "locks" (which also apply to ankles and feet), and elbow "lock-outs," which are also known as the "Arm-Bar" (which can also be used to lock-out the knee).

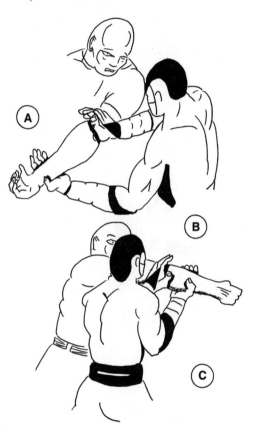

46. "Arm-Bar"

A. Having secured a hold on your opponent's wrist or forearm, rotate his arm to expose his elbow.
B. Attack into your foe's exposed elbow with a striking/pressing Palm-Strike.
C. Augment this Arm-Bar with leg-sweeps designed to topple your foe to the ground.

Strangleholds: Having seized a hold of our attacker, it's a simple matter to shift-pivot him into a stranglehold where you can literally choke the fight—and perhaps the life!—out of him with your hands, forearms, and, to a lesser extent, your legs.

Any forceful restriction on a foe's neck (cutting off blood flow/oxygen to the brain) sends him spiraling into unconciousness within thirty seconds.

Ninja grapplers learn strangleholds both for use in taking out sentries during field combat operations and when fighting face to face with a foe.

47. "Half-Strangle" Takedown

A. Having deflected your foe's right hand punching attack inward with your left Cross-Body Palm-Block, simultaneously slide your right arm under his attacking arm, up and around his neck.

B. "Catch" your right encircling arm with your left hand behind your foe's head, trapping him.

C. Augment this technique by using a "Kick-Back" sweep to topple him to the ground.

For example, during the initial clash with a foe, it is a simple matter to block/strike his attacking arm and easily slip yourself into a "Half-Strangle" takedown.

Likewise, we can seize him with a "Twist-Down," seizing hold on his hair or clothing and levering him into a stranglehold.

48. "Twist-Down" Takedown

A. Having blocked your foe's right punching attack with your right Palm-Up Block, rebound off his blocked arm, turning your Palm-Up Block into a Palm-Strike targeting his chin. Having struck his chin, seize a hold on his chin.
B. Simultaneously, grab a hold on your foe's hair, pulling with this grip while simultaneously pushing with your chin-hold.
C. Twist your foe back and down.
D. Augment this Twist-Down technique by pivoting back and away from your toppling foe.

49. "Yoke-n-Choke Strangle"

A. Your right arm encircles your foe's throat, your forearm *slams* back into his throat, constricting/crushing his larynx.

B. Simultaneously, drop your left arm down on the opposite side of his neck . . .

C. Lock your left hand onto the wrist/forearm of your right arm to complete this stranglehold.

D. Augment this technique by dropping your weight down and forward, placing even more pressure on your victim's neck.

Care must be taken never to leave yourself open to a counterattack while applying your stranglehold. For example, use the two-handed "Tiger's Mouth" strike-strangle only after an initial strike to his throat and to the base of the skull.

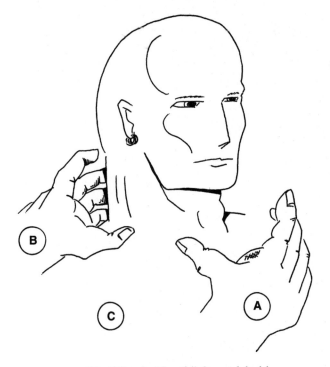

50. "Tiger's Mouth" Stranglehold

A. Having maneuvered to the side of your foe, slam your right "Tiger's Mouth" Strike into your foe's throat. Immediately on making contact, seize a grip on his larynx.

B. Simultaneously, strike into the base of his skull (Atlas & Axis) with an identical Tiger's Mouth Strike.

C. Follow through with a "Twist-down" pivot similar to that in illustration 48.

Ropes, electrical cords, wire, length of cloth, and a hundred other tools are used as impromptu strangling weapons by Ninja assassins.* For example, the Ninja sword scabbard (or any length of pipe or stout stick) can be used (see illustration 51, next page).

---

*The uncontested masters of the strangler's art are the *Thuggee,* who terrorized India well up into the nineteenth century. For a comprehensive history and complete training course in *Thuggee* combat, read Lung, 1995.

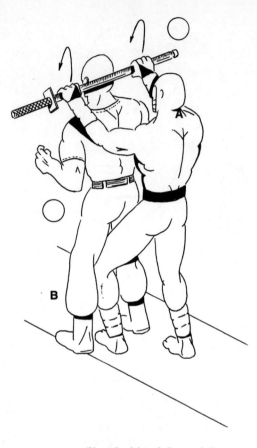

51. "Scabbard Strangle"

A. Drop the scabbard (stick, etc.) over your foe's head, jerking it back *violently* to damage/crush the larynx and/or stifle outcry.

B. Augment this move by kneeing up into the victim's crotch from behind to further upset his balance.

Grappling Rules. Grappling Rule #1: Having "bridged the gap" between you and your foe, with a foe, *stay in contact* either by "collapsing" into him with a succession of counterstrikes and/or by applying a grappling move to take him down and out. Reasoning: Recall the "Kick on the break" rule? Moving away from a foe once you've "closed" with him provides an opening into which he can strike.

Grappling Rule #2: *Never hold!* Having successfully trapped your attacker's arm or leg, *break it!* Reasoning: A wild animal caught in a snare will chew off its leg to escape certain death at the hands of the approaching hunter. Likewise, even when held in a painful, potentially maiming arm-lock, a desperate man (or one high on crack!) will still try to fight his way free. Better to lose your arm than your life, huh?

———

Where your safety and the safety of your loved ones is concerned, always assume your enemy is a "wild animal" . . . and treat him as such!

If such "tough" talk threatens your comfortable white bread, couch-potato world . . . *Good!*

In case you've been living in a cave in Afghanistan for the past couple of years and haven't heard, we're living in especially troubling times. Steel yourself to do what must be done.

Having chosen a lawless, heartless path, your foe forfeits his right to both pity and mercy.

On the other hand, having chosen to "study to survive," *you* can feel free to proudly reclaim and loudly proclaim the right of you and your seed to inherit the earth!

Investing in Loss. The first lesson a good guerilla fighter learns is how to "get ground by giving ground," for example, to pretend to flee to draw his enemy into an ambush.

Basic Sun Tzu. In Jujutsu, this is known as "investing in loss": Your opponent pushes, you pull. He pulls, you push.

Your foe rushes forward in a rage, you calmly shift, seize, pull, and pivot . . . and he goes flying (see *The Three Shifts*, next section).

This Push-Pull-Pivot strategy allows Ninja to outmaneuver and/or upset an opponent of any size. A perfect example of this is the "Wheel Throw":

52. "Wheel Throw" Takedown

Having seized a hold on your opponent's upper body (clothing, long hair), kick into his midsection with a Forward Thrust Kick (see illustration 25).

Groundwork. When shopping for a good martial arts school, one emphasizing the "martial" part, ask the instructor to show you his (or her) "groundwork," that is, how they fight (survive!) when they are knocked to the ground. If the instructor smirks, "Our fighters *never* get knocked down" . . . then don't put your money down.

"Groundwork"—learning to fight while on the ground and/or while your foe is on the ground—is as simple as who's on the ground? You or him?

The following three "Groundwork" rules are:

Groundwork Rule #1: When he's on the ground: *Finish Him!* (If stomping a man while he's down offends your sensibilities, you better hope your foe feels the same way when he has *you* on the ground and the shoe is on the other foot . . . and *in your face!*)

Groundwork Rule #2: When *you* are the one on the ground, get up ASAP!

Groundwork Rule #3: If unable to get back on your feet immediately, *actively fight from the ground,* kicking and trapping your foe's leg.

Groundwork Rule #4: *Fill your fist* any time your hand touches the ground. Snatch up a rock, stick, a handful of sand, *anything and everything* that can be used as an "environmental weapon" (see The Fourth Hall: Combat with "Flex-Ten Weapons").*

---

*As with most things in life, women are the exception when it comes to fighting on the ground, where it is often to a woman's advantage to delay a mugger (until help can arrive) by fighting from a prone position. Also, Nature has gifted women with natural lower body strength (i.e., broader hips), perfect for pivoting on the ground and for throwing powerful kicks. Female Ninja *Kuniochi* are expected to master this type of groundfighting and you will find such fighting taught by all *realistic* martial arts/self-defense courses.

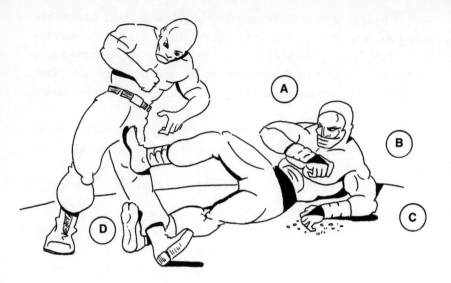

53. "Groundfighting"

A. Immediately after going to the ground, guard your upper body by placing your arm across your chest and raising one leg into defensive position (capable of kicking).

B. Use your other arm to help you maneuver (slide around and pivot on your hip) on the ground.

C. Ninja Rule: Any time your hand touches the ground FILL IT (e.g., with a rock, sand, dirt, a stick, etc.).

D. Use one leg to "trap," that is, pull and sweep your attacker's feet out from under him, while using your other leg to kick and "lock-out" his knees.

Note: Anytime you are knocked to the ground, job one is getting back to your feet.

Techniques

Martial arts is 90 percent *positioning*.

When attacked, we must instantly move ourselves "out of the line of fire" while simultaneously maneuvering ourselves into a "safe" and advantageous position from which to easily and effectively strike back into our opponent.

How and where we are standing when confronted determines *how* we respond. For example, "shifting" to one side or the other to avoid a punching attack means the difference between positioning yourself for an effective counterstrike on the one hand, or else inadvertently moving into your attacker's *second* punch or follow-up kick!

On the other hand, what if you "squat" in and under his blow instead of shifting? This response opens up completely different counterattack targets on your foe's body.

Therefore, your *stance,* how you use *shifting,* and the other "methods of movement" you use to position yourself before and during a confrontation determine whether you win or lose.

While there seem to be an endless number of combinations when it comes to moving into, away from, and avoiding an attacker, Ninja instructors in the First Hall early on isolated the few universal "methods of movement" that *all* the seemingly different schools of unarmed combat combine to accomplish specific results.

By learning to recognize and by sweating to "master" these "simple" methods of movement, the Ninja is always able to position himself so as to, first, evade his foe's assault, before then counterstriking back into his foe with devastating results.

THE THREE STANCES

How you stand—with legs flexed or with knees "locked," with your weight on one foot as opposed to the other—restricts your movement options.

Despite all the fancy "animal" stances we see in martial arts movies, the design of the human body restricts and requires a fighter to balance his weight in one of three stances:

Front Stance (aka an "Attack Stance"). Weight is distributed 70 percent on his forward-leading leg, 30 percent on his rear/tailing leg. When in this stance, your foe can only kick with his *rear* leg.

Back Stance (aka "Defense Stance"). Weight 70 percent on his rear leg, 30 percent on his front, your foe can only kick with his leading leg.

Even Stance (aka "Horse Stance"). His weight evenly distributed, *he cannot kick with either leg* until he shifts his weight one way or the another (into a Front Stance or a Back Stance).

54. "The Three Stances"

A. Back Stance (aka "Defensive Stance")
B. Even Stance (aka "Horse Stance")
C. Front Stance (aka "Attack Stance")

Always move toward and attack into your foe's "full" leg, the leg that is carrying most of his weight.

An experienced fighter will wait till an opponent shifts to a "Horse Stance" (weight evenly distributed) to strike knowing that his kicking ability will be restricted.

You can also attack when you see an opponent in a Front Stance—when you realize his lead leg is no danger to you.

THE TEN DIRECTIONS

It might seem that human beings have an unlimited number of choices when it comes to which direction to move. Were this true, we'd have no way to predict which direction our foe was about to move during a fight.

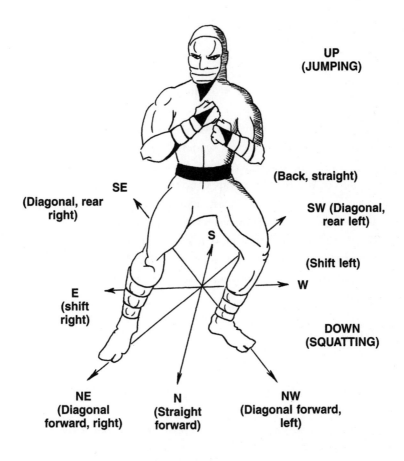

55. "The 10 Directions of Moving"

Fortunately, whether fighting or simply going about our every-day activities, human beings are all restricted to only *ten* directions of movement, corresponding to the eight directions on a compass, plus ducking and squatting "down" and leaping "up," to avoid a low-level attack (e.g., "sweep") or to jump over an obstacle.

It stands to reason then that in a combat situation, we have the option of moving forward (straight or diagonally), stepping back (straight or diagonally), shifting side to side, squatting or ducking to avoid a swinging-in strike, or else jumping up (and over) any-thing (kick or stick) threatening our legs.

While this might sound like your options are limited—they are!—take heart. These are also the directions of movement your foe is limited to.

Thus, with a minimum of study and a maximum of attention, it is relatively easy for the Ninja student—you—to spot a foe's inad-vertent clues: observing his stance, how he holds his hands, and so on, which of the ten directions your foe will move into next. With practice, you will be able to anticipate which direction he is going to jump *before* he consciously makes up his mind!

Ninja students acquire this skill by first becoming aware of their own shifting from stance to stance, especially how we *instinctually* move and guard ourselves when threatened by certain dangers (see *Blocking*).

THE THREE SHIFTS

Faced with a head-on assault, rather than "backpedal" the Ninja warrior "shifts" his "body profile" (silhouette) out of the line of fire by using one of the following movements:

Diagonal Shift (aka "Spear Shift"). Move forward at right or left angles to your foe's attacking arm or leg.

Simultaneous with your Diagonal Shifting, strike into his attack-ing arm with a "Cross-Body Block" while counterattacking into his "centerline."

56. "The Diagonal Shift"

A. Blocking your opponent's right punching attack . . .
B. Shift forward diagonally, to the outside of his punching arm.

Heel Shift (aka "Chinese Shift"). Without moving, twist/shift your weight onto your leg furthest from your attacker, while turning your lead leg onto its heel, thus avoiding your foe's punch.

Augment this shift with a cross-body block and with a counter-strike into his centerline.

57. "The Chinese Shift" (aka "Heel Shift")

A. As your attacker punches, block his attacking arm with both palms . . .

B. Simultaneously, shift 80 percent of your weight to the leg on the same side as his attacking arm, shifting weight off your opposite leg, and shifting to the side, away from his attacking arm.

Even Shift (aka "Horse Shift"). Moving back and away from your foe's attacking arm or leg, pick up your leading leg and place it down to the rear, forming a "Horse Stance." Note: This movement cuts your "body profile" in half, making you a more difficult target to hit.

Do not "land" stiff-legged, with knees "locked." Land with legs "flexed," like well-oiled springs. "Bounce" off these "springs" back into your foe with a devastating counterattack.

58. "The Horse Shift" (aka "Ever Swift")

As your opponent attacks with a punch or a kick, take yourself out of the line of fire by sliding your foot back and around, until you are "facing" your opponent in a side-forward stance (see illustrations 60, 62, and 63).

"HALF-MOON STEPPING"

When attacking or defending forward or to the rear, to the un-trained eye it appears Ninja move straight forward or straight back, a straight line. But in reality, Ninja always step in a "Half-Moon" step, slightly swinging their lead-moving leg in toward the other leg, before setting it out and down into a firm stance.

Note: Hidden within this Half-Moon stepping method is a "Reap" takedown, a sweeping foot maneuver that places you in position to sweep your opponent's feet out from under him.

Nearly all Ninja Unarmed Combat *Taijutsu* techniques have sim-ilar "hidden" and "secret" moves (see Lung and Prowant, 2000).

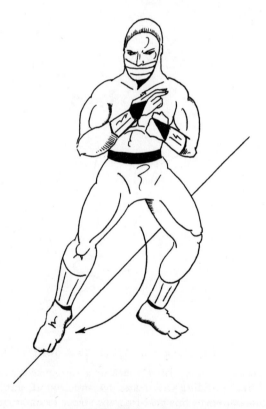

59. "Half-Moon Stepping"

"Crossing"

When you and your opponent face off with shoulders squared with one another, and your "centerline" is aligned with his, we call this being "boxed up." In this position, all your opponent's weapons (e.g., hands and feet) can easily reach you.

60. "Boxed Up"

Fighters with "boxed up" shoulders, torso, and hips, that is, their bodies aligned. From this position, your enemy can bring all his weapons (hands and feet) into play against you.

However, as soon as you adopt a side-oriented stance (i.e., with one hand leading, one side more toward your foe), your "body profile" (silhouette) is effectively cut in half, cutting down on the number of targets your foe can hit on you.

61. "Thinking Outside the Box"

Stepping back or otherwise shifting out of the "shoulders aligned" position makes you less of a target and prevents your opponent from using all his body weapons (see also illustrations 56–58).

Advance and "Cross" into your opponent by moving *forward* "crossing" his "centerline." As you move forward, *"fold"* (raise) your leading leg. This "folded" position protects your groin and lower body from your foe's defensive strikes as you are moving toward him.

From this "cocked" (folded) position, it is a simple matter of extending/snapping your folded leg out into a "Thrusting" or a "Crescent Kick."

(LINE OF ATTACK)

62. "Crossing-Over I"

A. "Boxed up" with your opponent, you move your body across the "Line of Attack" by folding your knee inward as you turn your body across the "Line of Attack."

B. From this "fold position" you are free to employ a kick (e.g., "Roundhouse"), a Horizontal Knee Strike, or to place your foot down on the opposite side of the "Line of Attack," into a more advantageous position for counterattacking (see illustration 63).

You can also achieve this "Crossing" side-stance positioning by performing a "Horse Shift," by stepping back into a "Back-Defensive Stance" or a "Horse Stance."

63. "Crossing-Over II"

You can also "cross-over" the center "Line of Attack" by stepping backward with a "Horse Shift" (see illustration 58).

"OVER-THE-FENCE"

A variation of "crossing" requires picking up your rear/trailing leg to pivot 180 degrees as you lash out with a "Spinning" Back-Fist strike and/or with an "Outside Cresent Kick."

While this move might at first appear "fancy" and daunting, it is as simple as raising your foot to "hop" over a short foot-high picket fence (hence its name).

64. "Over-the-Fence" Attacking

A. Pivoting on your leading leg, fold and raise the knee of your back leg as you pivot (as if to avoid a short fence or other low obstacle in your way) . . .

B. Once your folded leg passes over the imaginary "fence," snap your leg outward into an Outside Crescent Kick.

C. In lieu of striking with your foot, set your foot down "on the other side of the fence." Remember: Always land with a hand!

D. This method of movement also lends itself to a Spinning Backfist attack.

"THROUGH-THE-ARCH"

Still another "Method of Movement" technique designed to place you into a "safer" position from which to counterattack into your foe is called "Through-the-Arch."

Successfully executing this maneuver places you in a prime position, opening up multiple targets on your foe's (now) exposed centerline.

Targeting

Having absorbed the "tools" and "techniques" available to us, we continue our training in the First Hall by taking our unarmed combat training to the next level: "Targeting."

We've already acquired explosive striking power by following the "Form + Speed = Power" formula (review: *Developing Explosive Speed and Power*).

"Targeting" goes beyond learning to strike/counterstrike with focus and ferocity into chosen targets on our foe's body.

"Targeting" refers to the ability to respond instantly, correctly, without inhibiting thought. Masters often describe this effect as an almost "out-of-the-body" experience, as if they are "watching" their bodies fight.

When "targeting," your striking hand, foot, or other body tool literally "leaps" forward of its own volition to strike just the right target on your foe's body to achieve maximum effect.

With "targeting," you "watch" as your defending/attacking tool instantly "bounces" off your foe's limb. But instead of retracting (like a Western boxer's punch), immediately on making contact, your blocking/attacking arm or leg "bounces" off your foe's limb like it was bouncing off a diving board, to "spring" forward, counterattacking into vulnerable targets in one smooth, *fluid motion*.

Fluid motion, "flow," facilitates force.

Two practices that aid us in acquiring "targeting" ability are *Rebounding* and *The Collapsing Principle*.

REBOUNDING

The best illustration of "Rebounding" is the way *nunchakus* (aka "numb-chucks") operate. All those spectacular spinning moves done by experts swinging nunchakus are actually "rebounding" moves.

Having struck with one end of the weapon, nunchakus instantly "bounce" back off the struck target, too quickly for the wielder to check its momentum. To control the nunchaku, the rebounding end is allowed to circle up and around or down and around until it slaps into the wielder's other waiting hand, from which he can then continue his attack *without retracting or stopping/restarting* his weapon.

This same "bouncing off," that is, *Rebounding* principle, is used with other martial arts weapons, such as *jo*-short sticks and the *bo*-staff (see The Second Hall: Combat with Wooden Weapons).

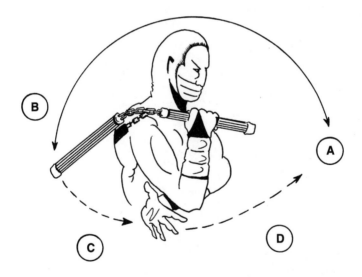

65. "Numb-Chucks Rebounding"

A. As "numb-chucks" strike an object (e.g., collarbones) . . .
B. They rebound . . .
C. Necessitating catching them on the rebound . . .
D. So as to reroute their continuing force, rather than trying to stop and restart them each time.

In the same way, rather than retracting/rechambering your hand after striking a foe, or when your initial strike has been blocked or otherwise diverted, *don't retract, rebound!* Allow your hand to "bounce" off his blocking hand, whipping around into another exposed target.

Visualize your hand bouncing off and then whipping around his blocking arm the way rushing water whips around a rock in its path.

For example, finding his initial Back-Fist attack blocked, the Ninja instantly bounces off the blocking arm, turning his Back-Fist strike into a "Snake-Punch."

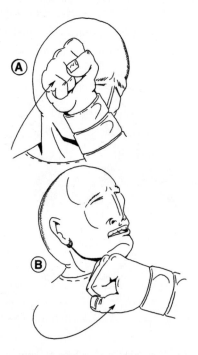

66. "Snake-Punch" Rebound

A. Having struck your opponent on the temple with a solid Back-fist Strike . . .
B. Rebounding from your initial strike, use the added momentum to whip your fist around, striking upwards with a two-knuckle Snake-Punch.

The best exercise for developing hand rebounding is the traditional *Kan-Ryu Yo-te*, "Four Hands" exercise.

67. "Yo-Te" Four-hand Striking

**Punch downward, targeting the lower abdomen with a "Chinese Fist"
(see illustration 17).**

We'll return to this "basic" Four-Hand pattern in both the Second and Third Halls.

THE COLLAPSING PRINCIPLE

The second exercise required for mastering the skill of targeting is "The Collapsing Principle."

68. "The Collapsing Principle"

As you make contact with your foe, rather than withdraw your initial hand and/or foot strike to strike again, "collapse" into your opponent, hitting him with a succession of blows:

A. Spearhand (finger stabs) collapse into . . .
B. Fist strikes collapse into . . .
C. "Crane's Head" wrist strikes collapse into . . .
D. Forearm strikes collapse into . . .
E. "Shortwing" Elbow strikes collapse into . . .
F. Shoulder strikes collapse into . . .
G. Head butts collapse into . . .
H. Biting attacks.
I. Long-range kicking attacks collapse into . . .
J. Knee strikes collapse into . . .
K. Sweeps with the foot and shin collapse into . . .
L. Hip throws.

Having made initial contact with your foe, for example, having struck him with a solid hand blow, instead of retracting your striking hand, "collapse" into him, "following through" with any number of strikes: Wrist strike, Forearm blow, or Elbow strike.

This "Collapsing Principle" also works with kicking techniques (see illustration 13).

While "Rebounding" and "The Collapsing Principle" are very real *physical* tactics and techniques, as with all things in the Shinobi realm, these two principles harbor a deeper, *philosophical* insight: one that teaches the Ninja to *always be flexible* by using mental "rebounding" and, rather than shirk back from life, to "collapse" forward into life, embracing challenge and even conflict as our best opportunities to "test" our shining metal—both that in our scabbard and the mettle of our heart and determination.

Special Note: Having mastered—or at least *survived!*—unarmed combat training in the First Hall, we now proceed to Halls Two through Five, where we will familiarize ourselves with the use of the myriad of weapons available to the Ninja—for both defense and offense.

Despite your sucesses so far, you may still feel some trepidation. After all, Ninja are known—okay, universally *feared!*—for their fantastic arsenal of weapons; for their mastery of traditional weapons, as well as their use of improvised "environmental weapons," not the least of which is their "magical" ability to produce weapons seemingly out of thin air.

Don't worry. Worry is that most wasteful of emotions.

Having already learned the targets and having mastered the fundamental strikes and methods of movement required of students in the First Hall, *you already know how to use Ninja weapons!*

Thus, in the following weapons-oriented halls, you must *learn to recognize and concentrate on the similarities* between those unarmed movements you already know and those weapons tactics and techniques you will be required to master to survive training in these "weapons halls."

A pencil is just a pencil until *you* decide it is a dagger!

⚡ ⚡ ⚡

PYO,
"The Great Diamond,"

grants the seeker the attribute of *focus*

and opens the way to entrance into

THE SECOND HALL:
COMBAT WITH WOODEN WEAPONS

INTRODUCTION: *"COMBAT WITH WOODEN WEAPONS"*

WOODEN WEAPONS WERE ONE OF THE FIRST WEAPONS EARLY man used to coldcock his less-evolved brethren. Mother Nature rewards inventive-minded DNA.

Today, a good solid Louisville Slugger is still a dependable reasoning tool when negotiating with Neanderthals.

Knowing this, Shinobi Ninja used all the traditional wooden weapons of their time, while going out of their way to develop new variations on these tried-and-true standbys.

As masters of unarmed combat, Ninja realized early on that the secret to mastering any weapon was to keep in mind that *weapons are but an extension of the human body.*

As such, weapons accomplish three primary purposes:

- ◆ *Weapons extend our reach,* allowing us to strike an enemy from further distant; from a short fighting-stick extending our reach a few inches, to medieval longbows, down through a modern sniper rifle (or better yet, an unmanned, remote-control Predator flying drone!) that extends our "reach" even further.
- ◆ *Weapons reinforce and increase our striking power.* For example, any small object (e.g., roll of quarters, small stones) gripped firmly in hand increases the impact of our striking fist.
- ◆ *Weapons scare the hell out of people!* The sudden appearance of a weapon, even a small penknife, changes the whole complexion of a fight, often literally changing the complexion of a cowardly attacker, especially one unschooled in the use of weapons.

Individuals untrained in weapons use all too often give more credit (i.e., fear) to weapons than they deserve.

In an emergency, simply picking up a sharp stick or two-by-four can make an already cowardly mugger beat feet (more on such "environmental weapons" in the Fifth Hall: Specialized Combat Training).

The keenest of knives in the hands of a knave is but a bluff. The dullest of pencils in the hands of a schooled assassin can still write your epitaph.

The man makes the weapon, the weapon does not make the man.

Ninja Rule: Fight the man, not the weapon.

Ninja used a bevy of wooden weapons, each of which fit the three criteria outlined earlier.

San-jo, the Three Sticks

Shinobi were masters of a myriad of simple wooden weapons, as well as wood-based weapons augmented with metal blades, chains, and other nasty surprises.

The three basic wooden fighting tools of the Ninja are the yawara (fitting in the palm of the hand), the *jo* short-stick (roughly the length from fingertips to elbow), and the *bo*-staff (ideally, the length from floor to chin, although some schools prefer the bo-staff to extend to the forehead or even longer).

YAWARA (AKA KOBUTON)

Approximately five-inches in length, the yawara not only strengthens the fist for striking, its ends—extending slightly from the hand—can be used for striking, for example, using the same *Yo-te* striking shown in illustration 68.

Commercial models of the yawara are sold as convenient key-chain attachments. In the same self-defense vein, some commercial pepper-spray containers have been slimmed down so they can pull double duty as a yawara stick.

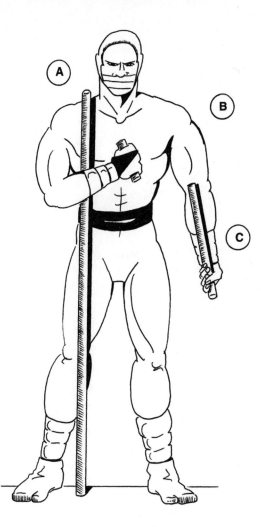

69. "San-Jo," the Three Sticks

A. The bo-staff should come up to your chin.
B. The jo-stick should reach from your palm to your elbow.
C. The yawara should extend slightly beyond the ends of your palm (see illustration 71).

70a. "Yawara" Striking (Yo-Te II)
Using the Yo-Te exercise from illustration 63, strike forward and
down, targeting your opponent's solar plexus and/or abdomen.

70b.
Rebounding off your initial abdomen blow, strike up into your
opponent's temple by swinging the yawara first inward (across your
centerline) and then up and outward, targeting his temple.

In an emergency, any pencil, pen, or utensil of similar length can be used as an "environmental weapon" yawara.

JO-STICK

Schools of short-stick fighting are found in cultures worldwide, from Engligh *Singlestick* to Filipino *Escrima*, to Vietnamese *Chong-gay* (Lung, 2003:179).

Any solid short-stick (length of pipe, etc.) can be used to block hand strikes and kicks and/or to reinforce your blocking arm.

Jo-sticks can also be used to strike into the same targets in the same manner as with unarmed strikes. For example, the *Yo-te* rebounding exercise you're already familiar with (illustration 68) can easily be adapted for stick use.

BO-STAFF

Some form of staff-fighting is found in all ancient cultures. Primitively, these "long-sticks" were sharpened to a point and hardened with fire. Later, sharpened flint and ultimately metal spearpoints were added.

At its simplest, any sturdy length of stick, board, or pipe can be used to block and "ward off" an attacker.

In addition, the bo-staff can be used to strike into the same targets as your unarmed strikes.

Ninja often augmented their (hollow) "walking staffs" with a multitude of hidden weapons.

Additional Wooden Weapons

People still argue whether the realistic-looking pistol the bank robber John Dillenger used to escape from the Crown Point, Indiana, jail was carved out of soap or wood. Regardless, Dillenger's ploy worked.

We do know for sure that, besides *San-jo* weapons, Ninja developed a bevy of other wooden weapons. These included:

71. "Jo-stick Reinforces Arm"

A. Having used the jo-stick to reinforce your arm (e.g., Rising Block) . . .

B. Follow-through by counterattacking with the jo-stick.

72. Jo-stick Attacking

Any sturdy length of stick (pipe, etc.) can be used to:

A. Strike bludgeon-like . . .
B. Stab/Thrust . . .
C. Unbalance and sweep an enemy.

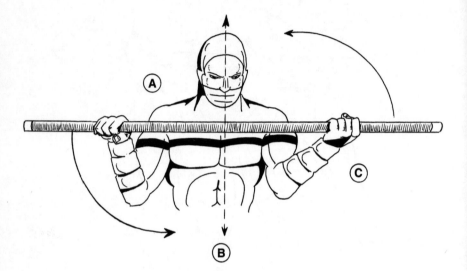

73. "Bo-Staff Wall of Iron" Blocking

A. Block Forward with the bo-staff by thrusting it forward.
B. Block high-level punches and/or low-level kicks by sliding the bo-staff up and down.
C. Turn aside attacks coming at you from left and/or right by rotating the bo.

74. "Defensive/Offensive Response (Unarmed)"
Deflect your attacker's punch with a Palm-Up Block

75. "Defensive/Offensive Response (Armed with Bo)"

Following the same defensive/offensive pattern you used when unarmed:

A. Use your bo-staff to deflect your attacker's arm down and inward . . .

B. Having deflected your attacker's arm, strike up into his face . . .

C. Having struck his face, your bo rebounds off its target and "leaps" over his head to strike into the base of his skull (Atlas & Axis) . . .

D. Rebounding off the blow to the base of his skull, circle your bo-staff down to sweep his legs from behind.

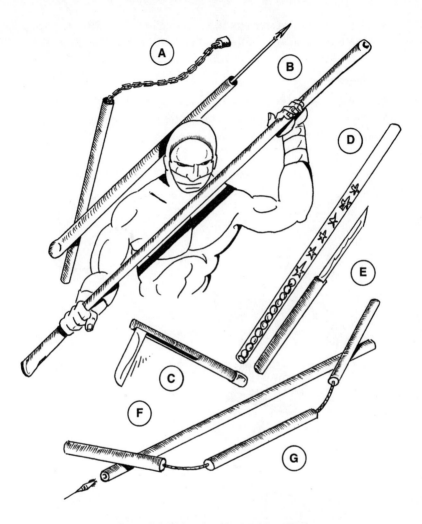

76. Ninja "Walking Staff" Hidden Weapons

A. Manariki-weighted chain
B. Arrow-spear (fired by spring or by gunpowder)
C. Folding Kama-sickle
D. Calatrops and other Tonki designed to trip up and unbalance pursuers
E. Miscellaneous blades
F. Blowgun
G. Nunchakus and three-sectioned Chinese Fighting Staff

- *Tonfa,* which Westerners insist on called the "PR-24," originated in Okinawa, before being adopted by Japanese Ninja who often augmented this wooden weapon with hidden blades.
- *Blowguns* capable of firing poison-tipped darts.
- *Wooden Sword Scabbards,* which often doubled as a blowgun, and could be used to strangle a sentry.

Besides being used to augment unarmed fighting techniques, wooden weapons could be used for a variety of uses.

77. "Additional Ninja Wooden Weapons"

A. Scabbard used as a blowgun (see illustration 51)
B. Body-armor (abdomen, forearms, shins, etc.)
C. Tonfa (Okinawan variation of jo-fighting stick)

- *Armor*, used to reinforce forearms, worn under clothing to protect against stabbing attacks. FYI: Most Samurai armor was made of wood.
- *Booby traps*, for example, the type of *punji* stick traps made infamous by the Viet Cong.

See also the Fourth Hall: Flex-Ten Weapons using wooden weapons, and Fifth Hall, "Special Weapons."

78. "Wooden Field Booby Traps"

SHA,
"The Pure Wind,"

grants the seeker the attribute of *healing*

and opens the way to entrance into

THE THIRD HALL:
COMBAT WITH BLADED WEAPONS

INTRODUCTION: *"DOES SIZE MATTER?"*

Ninja bladed weapons meet the three criteria Ninja demand of all their weapons:

- Bladed weapons *extend our reach*—swords and blade-tipped spears, for example, as well as bladed *throwing* weapons.
- Bladed weapons can *reinforce striking power.* For example, you can strike with the pommel of a heavy knife or sword, while merely gripping the hilt can strengthen a (Back) Fist blow.
- Finally, knives and other blades *scare the hell out of people!* Even an enemy who will foolishly try to wrestle a pistol from you will often hesitate at grabbing for a knife, knowing that their least miscalculation, or the merest flick of your wrist, can cause them to lose a finger—if not their life.

Blades are figuratively and literally more primitive than firearms and thus invoke more "primitive" reactions from those facing such weapons.

Another advantage blades have over more complex weapons like firearms is that metal blades (and other cutting and stabbing tools) are easy to come by in almost any environment, from your grandmother's living room (see Omar, 1993) to weapons hidden inside a government prison cell (see Omar, 2001).

Don't feel overwhelmed by the number of bladed weapons available to you. In the same vein, don't allow yourself to be confused by the *seeming differences* among all the different sizes and types of bladed weapons.

Look for the similarities—similarities in ways of wielding different types of blades, similarities in how the handling of bladed weapons is akin to throwing unarmed blows and to handling wooden weapons, and, as we will learn in the Fourth Hall, similarities in handling "flexible" weapons.

Types of Bladed Weapons

Bladed weapons come in all shapes and sizes. While the uninitiated might at first think that "the bigger the blade the better," vetted Ninja know that a small blade often has advantages over a longer, more apparent weapon.

If you doubt the power inherent in small-bladed weapons, recall what a few fanatics armed with only box cutters were able to accomplish on September 11, 2001 (see *Kakashi-jutsu*, below).

SWORDS (AKA NINPO)

As a rule, Ninja swords are shorter than traditional Samurai *katana*. In addition, Ninja do not "worship" their swords as "sacred" as did/do Samurai. For Ninja, the sword is just another tool for accomplishing an end . . . the end of their enemies!

Ninja swords were generally crafted of less-quality metal (more iron than steel) than Samurai swords. The blades of Ninja swords were smoked black, to help avoid detection.

Ninja swords were primarily stabbing weapons, their lengths purposely left dull so the sword could be used for climbing. In the same vein, the hilt of the Ninja sword was purposely large, also to facilitate climbing, for example, used for a step when propped against a wall.

While balanced, the handle of the sword was sometimes hollowed out and used to carry poisons, darts, or a thin rope.

The scabbard (usually made of wood) could double as a snorkel or as a blowgun and was usually longer than the sword itself, its tip being used to store small objects.

Shinobi even developed a firearm they cleverly disguised as a hilted sword.

KNIVES (AKA TANTO)

Ninja don't carry "fighting knives," they carry "killing knives." A "knife fight" is a sign of poor planning. Your enemy should never see the knife that kills him.

For Ninja, the knife was not only a handy tool for sentry removal but also a useful tool for digging and prying open doors, and so on.

Like the sword, the Ninja knife was primarily a stabbing weapon, its edge often left dull. Ninja knives, some only a couple of inches long, others short swords, usually had heavy pommels so they could be used for striking.

Modern-day knives include "shooting knives," whose blades shoot out from the hilt driven by powerful springs or propelled by CO_2 gas. The effectiveness of these "shooting knives" varies greatly (see Lung, 1998).

When choosing a "killing knife," avoid knives with serrated edges, as these can all too easily get caught up in your victim's clothing . . . and his ribs!

Also avoid knives whose fancy hilts and handles cover your hand and/or require you to "trap" one or more of your fingers inside "rings" on the handle, the same way the trigger-guard of a pistol can trap your finger.

(For a complete training course in the use of knives, see Lung, 1997b.)

MIXED-BLADED WEAPONS

Mixed-bladed weapons are created when Ninja augment wooden weapons, for example, the bo-staff, with metal blades or "spear" points.

The best example of this is the Ninja's commonly used *Kama-*

sickle, consisting of a solid wood handle augmented with a thick blade protruding at a 90-degree angle.

79. "Kama-Sickle" (with Chain)

Kama were often further augmented with either rope or chain attachments that, technically, qualifies them as a "flexible weapon" (more on this in the Fourth Hall).

Ninja were also (in)famous for hiding blades inside innocent-looking wooden walking staffs, canes, scrolls, scabbards, and so on.

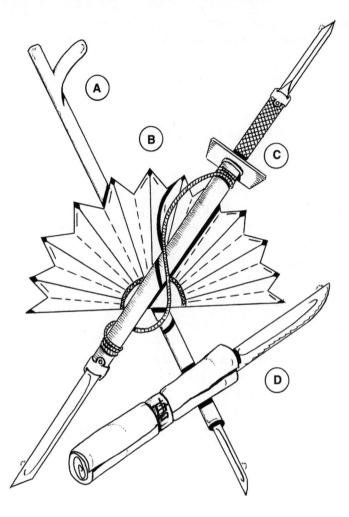

80. "Ninja Hidden Blades"

A. Inside walking canes (see illustration 77)
B. Fan with hidden blade edges
C. Ninja Tonpo-sword in scabbard, with blades that protrude when triggered (surprising opponent expecting you to have to "draw" your sword!)
D. Blade hidden inside message scroll (triggered by spring)

KAKASHI-JUTSU

To Japanese, Miyamoto Musashi, the author of the classic on strategy, *A Book of Five Rings* (1643), is *"Kensei"*, the "Sword Saint," universally acknowledged as the greatest swordsman who ever lived in Japan.

Ironically, many of Musashi's greatest victories were won, not with Samurai sword, but through Musashi's use of everyday "environmental weapons": his scabbard, a fan, tree limb, rowboat oar, even a cooking pot laddle.

Always unconventional, Musashi also took the time to master *Kakashi-jutsu*, the art of using small objects to defeat a foe.

Ninja class such small, easily hidden fighting tools under the catch-all *"tonki."*

Tonki include a wide variety of dirks, darts, calatrops, and the universally recognized *shuriken*, better known as the "Ninja star."

Most tonki are small enough to be hidden in the palm of the hand and/or avoid detection when hidden on your person. But don't let their size fool you. A three-inch blade can penetrate to nearly all vital organs and any small razor blade–like weapon is capable of cutting a throat (need we mention the September 11, 2001, box cutters again?).

Often coated with poison, calatrops and other small spikes can be littered on the ground behind you, thereby penetrating searchers' shoes. Still other blades can be attached (like booby-traps) to surfaces a pursuing enemy is likely to grab for—to trip up and dissuade pursuers.

Contrary to Hollywood, most Ninja "throwing stars" were not/ are not heavy enough to cause death by penetration. That's why, in medieval times, shuriken and other throwing tonki were poison-tipped.

Some tonki can be held in the hand for reinforcing the hand and/or for slashing (see *The Four Grips*, below).

How to Use Bladed Weapons

Once you familiarize yourself with the various types of bladed weapons available to us, we then master the various ways of wielding these weapons.

THE FOUR GRIPS
Bladed weapons can be held in one of four ways:

The Outside Grip is the most common way a person, especially an untrained person, holds a bladed weapon, in particular, a knife. This grip facilitates straight-in stabbing, horizontal slashing attacks, and "up the center" vertical cuts.

81. "Outside Knife Grip"

The Inside Grip "hides" the knife along the inside of the forearm. This grip facilitates horizontal slashing cuts and downward stabbing strikes.

The Thumb-Index Grip is similar to the "Outside Grip" except that it is used to grip smaller blades, the way you might hold a razor blade.

82. "Thumb-Index Grip"

"Spike-fist" allows a cutting or stabbing weapon to "protrude" out from between your fingers. So-called push knives (aka "T-knives") use this grip, as do certain dirks and "environmental weapons" such as pencils.

83. "Spike-Fist"

Once we've learned how to hold our bladed weapon(s), we then proceed to learn (1) how to strike and (2) where to strike.

HOW TO STRIKE

As with wooden weapons (illustration 73), the *Yo-te* "rebounding" exercise (illustration 68) can easily be adapted for use with various bladed weapons.

84. "Knife Striking" (Yo-Te III)

Using the Yo-Te exercise from illustration 68 (and 71), strike forward and down, targeting your enemy's solar plexus and/or abdomen.

Basically, there are only *three* directions from which a foe can attack you with a bladed weapon, and vice versa.

Straight-in, trusting-stabbing attack; knife (or other pointed weapon) held in an Outside Grip. Exception, stabbing backward (your back to your enemy) using an Inside Grip.

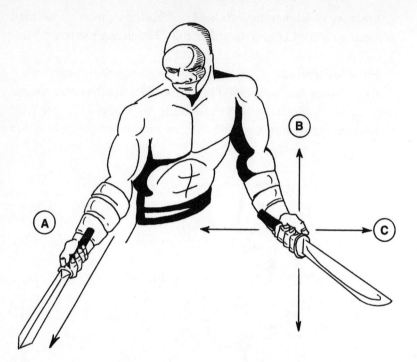

85. "Three Directions of Knife Attack"

A. Straight-in (forward) Thrust
B. Vertical (up and down) from either "inside" or "outside" grips.
C. Horizontal (side-to-side), includes "slashing."

Horizontal in-n-out, back-n-forth slashing. Outside Grip, you target the abdomen, Inside Grip, you slash across your enemy's throat.

Vertical, up and down slashing, with variations of *diagonal cutting* slashes. Inside Grip, you stab down into your enemy's collarbones and upper chest. With the Outside Grip you slash upward, targeting his centerline.

WHERE TO STRIKE

Despite movie depictions of Ninja swordfighting toe to toe with Samurai, this seldom happened in real life.

Ninja prefer striking unseen and/or from behind, taking out an enemy before that enemy has an inkling death is even in the building.

While any part of your enemy's body can be attacked by bladed weapons (review illustration 15), striking some targets, even with a blade, will only allow you to wound your enemy.

A wounded animal is all the more dangerous.

Other targets, for example, stabbing up into vital organs, kill instantly.

Still other targets will render your enemy unconscious within thirty seconds, dead within minutes, but still plenty long enough for him to kill you before he dies!

Where and how you strike into your enemy depends on (1) what type of bladed weapon(s) you have, and (2) what targets are immediately accessible to you.

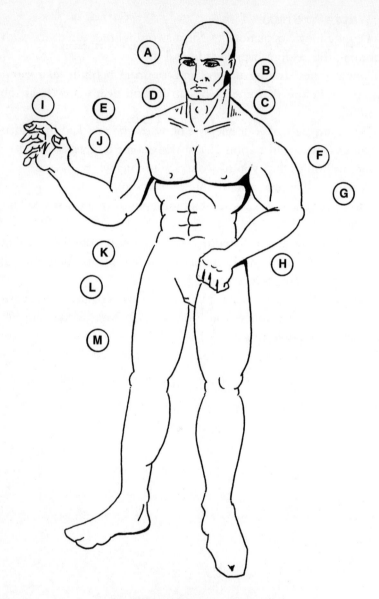

86. "Bladed Weapons Targets"

A. Face: Thrust into face. Through the eyes = kill shot.
B. Ears: Use "Ice-pick" dirk-skewers. Kill shot.

C. Neck: Stab and slash. Major arteries and veins near the surface. Possible kill shot.
D. Throat: Stab and slash directly into the throat, targeting the larynx. Kill shot.
E. Collarbones: Stab down inito this area to sever subclavian veins and arteries. Kill shot.
F. Armpit: Stab up into the armpit.
G. Arms: To sever muscles, ligaments, and tendons.
H. Wrists
I. Fingers
J. Solar plexus (stabbing, straight-in into heart and aorta)
K. Abdomen: Stabbing, "straight up the middle."
L. Groin: Stabbing attacks.
M. Inner Thigh: Stab and slice into femoral veins and arteries.

⚡ ⚡ ⚡

KAI,
"The Dragon's Hand,"

grants the seeker the attribute of *adaptability*

and opens the way to entrance into

THE FOURTH HALL:
COMBAT WITH "FLEX-TEN" WEAPONS

INTRODUCTION: *"FLEX-TEN WEAPONS"*

When you first hear it, "Flex-Ten weapons" sounds exotic. But have you ever flicked a gym buddy with a wet "rat-tail" towel? Ever used a rubberband to shoot a paperclip at a co-worker? If so, then you've already used "Flex-Ten"—flexible and tension—tools.

Flexible Weapons

Flexibility is the key to both physical and mental accomplishment. This is especially true when it comes to *Ninjutsu* training.

Mentally and physically, Ninja must always stay "flexible," learning to "think on their feet," to improvise, adapting instantly to changing circumstance and flux.

Not surprising then that Ninja should have mastered the art of "flexible weapons," all of which use "snapping" and/or "spinning" motions designed to take full adavantage of the laws of physics.

SNAPPING TOOLS

That rat-tail towel you used to torture your buddy is a good example of a "snapping" motion, as is a bullwhip and a "slap-jack" bludgeon, both of which get their power from snapping motions.

SPINNING TOOLS

Other Flexible Weapons gather force as they spin and, on striking an object, release their energy into that object. This is especially true of any cord, rope, chain, and so on that has a weight attached to one or both ends.

When watching martial arts masters "spin" weapons, for example, Okinawan nunchakus ("numb-chucks") and kama-sickles affixed with cords or chains, it appears as if there are an endless number of ways these flexible weapons can be spun. In actuality, 90 percent of these swinging moves and maneuvers boil down to "The Three-Eights": the Forward Eight, the Back Eight, and the Figure Eight, so-called because all three use an "8"-shaped movement:

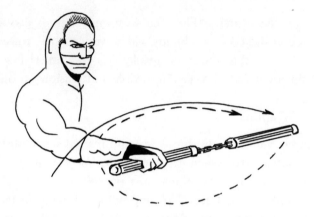

87a. "Nunchaku Attack I: Forward Eight"

Nunchaku circles forward, alternating circles pass on inside and outside of forearm

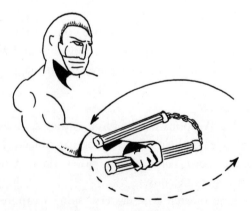

87b. Nunchaku Attack II: "Back Eight"

Nunchaku circles backward, alternating circles pass first on the inside and then the outside of the forearm.

Some flexible weapons use both snapping and spinning motions. The best example of this are "numb-chucks," which can both be "cast," that is, snapped into a target, as well as spun at terrific speeds into targets.

88. "Nunchaku Attack III: Casting"
(See also illustration 91.)

Other types of flexible weapons, those employing woven cords and chains, can also be used in both manners. For example, the manriki (weighted-chain, highly popular with Ninja for its easy concealability) can be used both as a snapping weapon and a spinning weapon.

Various impromtu "environmental weapons" also lend themselves to both snapping and spinning attacks. The best example is the popular prison weapon—"rock-in-a-sock" bludgeon (Omar, 2001).

More on "environmental weapons" in the Fifth Hall.

89. Easily concealed Manriki-chain weapon

Depending on the particular length and strength of the rope, cord, or chain used to craft the flexible weapon, flexible weapons can also be used to:

- Strangle a sentry
- Aid in climbing
- Set up booby-traps

Tension Weapons

Tension = potential energy. When that "tension" is properly aimed and loosed . . . things get broken and people get hurt. Our enemies, for example.

Various traditional Ninja weapons, as well as more exotic weapons worldwide, employ this tension principle. These include:

- ◆ Bows and crossbows
- ◆ Blowguns (dart propelled by pent-up air)
- ◆ "Wrist-Rocket" slingshots (using rubber tubing)
- ◆ Shooting knives (powered by springs)
- ◆ "Pelletguns" and dartguns (using CO_2 propellants)
- ◆ The Atlatl (short spear propelled by a "casting stick")

90. The Atlatl

Some *Ninjutsu* schools disagree whether *Ho-jutsu,* the study of firearms and explosives, belongs here in this hall or is more properly placed in the Fifth Hall: Specialized Combat Training.

Most Ninja *ryu* opt for assigning the study of firearms and explosives to the Fifth Hall, even though the very nature of explosives, including bullets, depend on the use of chemical "tension."

FYI: Denied more sophisticated weapons, prisoners often construct deadly "tension" weapons from innocuous objects such as woven rubberbands and even the elastic waistbands of their underwear (see Omar, 2001).

TOH,
"The Watercourse,"

grants the seeker the attribute of *balance*

and opens the way to entrance into

THE FIFTH HALL:
SPECIALIZED COMBAT TRAINING

INTRODUCTION: *"THE ENDLESS HALL"*

While the sign on the door reads: "Specialized Combat Training," what this hall truly specializes in is teaching Ninja "nonlinear thinking," that is, learning to use what we've already learned in the previous four halls in unconventional ways.

This hall also acts as a catch-all for specific—and often secret—skills and training methods unique to, and vital to, the mastery of *Ninjutsu*.

Who can predict what particular piece of data or what deadly dance of dagger we will need at any given time, some obscure physical skill, some impossible scheme of skulduggery, that will spell the difference between our being on time for our victory dinner or late for our own funeral!

And so . . . we learn it all! Or at least make sure that our "base" of overall knowledge is broad enough to accomodate the immediate acquisition of any new training and/or skills needed to accomplish today's mission.

This process of perpetual learning "ends" the day we die.

Thus, Ninja really do "learn something new every day"! Hence, "The Endless Hall."

Musashi commanded his students "Know the Ways of all professions" and in so doing, we better the odds that, when needed, that particular scheme or skill will already be waiting in our black bag of tricks.

And when need be, Ninja must remain humble enough to call in "specialists" for specific tasks, for example, someone familiar with the specific area, culture, or individual you intend to "penetrate."

Training and tactics stored in this hall are organized into three areas of concentration.

The first is "Specialized Methods of Movement," where we learn tactics and techniques *unique* to *Ninjutsu* study, ways of concealing our purpose while confusing the purpose of our foes'.

The second is "Specialized Weapons."

The third area of specialty concentrates on *Sennin-jutsu,* mind-manipulation techniques that penetrate our enemy's mind quicker and slicker than an icepick.

Specialized Methods of Movement

The word "ninja" is synonymous with "shadow and stealth" and, indeed, the Shinobi were masters of moving unseen, and not just when cloaked in darkness.

Ninja were also trained to travel unseen, thus unmolested, during the day, and to travel disguised through hostile territories. More on this in the Sixth Hall. (For a complete training course in "Shadow and Stealth," see Lung, 1998).

Necessity demanded that Ninja also master the art of escape and evasion (see the Eighth Hall).

And, at all times, Ninja knew the value of hiding both their intent as well as their actual weapons from their foes until the very instant of striking. This required Ninja disguising both their offensive and defensive unarmed and armed combat tactics and techniques from the enemy.

Ninja called these collective skills *Taisavaki,* literally, "The Art of Avoidance."

More commonly known as "Shadowhand," this is the ability to move unseen through hostile areas, to ingress and egress undetected, and, when need be, "vanish" in a puff of smoke. The Shadowhand credo: "Avoid being seen; seen, avoid capture; captured, avoid being held." (For a complete training course in Taisavaki see Lung and Prowant, 2000.)

Special Weapons

We've already seen how Ninja went out of their way to disguise their weapons (e.g. blades in *bo*-staff).

But, depending on the particular mission, Ninja were often called on to become craftsmen and artists (or to "contract" professional craftsmen) to create special weapons and devices designed (1) to get them close to their objective/target and (2) to help them accomplish/remove that objective.

This could be as simple as forging a convincing traveling permit, to forging a brilliant Samurai sword designed to dazzle, and thus get your deep-cover agent close to a targeted *Shogun* who collected such blades.

Stealing (or crafting) an *objet d'art* sure to catch the eye of the targeted person can get you close to that target and/or allow you to conceal an electronic bug, camera, or even an explosive device in the artwork. This is an excellent ploy when faced with an "inconsiderate" enemy who just flatly refuses to die from "natural causes" (like that block of *Semtex* you placed under his car seat!).

ENVIRONMENTAL WEAPONS

As your skill with weapons mastered in the first four halls increases, you'll naturally become more adept at spotting both innovative uses for those traditional wooden, bladed, and flexible/tension weapons, as well as ready substitutes for these weapons.

This is where "environmental weapons" come in.

Entering a heavily guarded castle where you are certain to be searched (and nowadays, electronically scanned), Ninja operatives must either (1) successfully hide undetectable weapons on their person and/or (2) have the acumen to gather and/or craft weapons from their immediate surroundings. Sometimes this means "borrowing" weapons from a lax enemy sentry who'll have no further use for them in the Afterlife . . . and/or gleaning "environmental weapons," those everyday objects that can be used in place of more traditional weapons.

The number of environmental weapons is endless.

Even guards in hi-tech "super-maximum security" prisons are hard-pressed to prevent prisoners from manufacturing weapons from objects as "innocent" as toothbrushes and plastic spoons (Omar, 2001).

Likewise, the average room in the average home houses hundreds if not thousands of environmental weapons you can use in an emergency (e.g., a home invasion) to protect yourself and your loved ones (Omar, 1993; Skinner, 1995).

Sennin-jutsu

We normally think of Ninja as warriors. But as in all armies, 90 percent of Ninja clan members acted as "support personnel," providing valuable intelligence and support equipment and supplies and helping other operatives get to and from the area of operations site.

Some Ninja acted as equipment specialists, obtaining and, where necessary, crafting the specialized equipment on-site field operative(s) needed to carry out their missions.

Still other Ninja were accomplished *shaman,* responsible for tending to both the physical (i.e., medical needs) of the clan as well as preparing those notorious poisons and other dubious concoctions so vital to Shinobi skulduggery.

While all Ninja students are expected to get more than just a little "Psych 101" under their sash, Ninja who specialized in attacking an enemy where he is most vulnerable—his mind—were known as *Sennin,* "Masters of the Mind."

Consummate psychologists, Sennins' insights into general human frailty and phobia were sharp enough to puncture even Freud's ego.

Accomplished Sennin helped plan the overall strategies of the clan, providing clan *Jonin* with invaluable insight into the thinking processes of the enemy. This included examining everything from an enemy's relationships to his family and leaders, to his superstitions (see the Ninth Hall), thereby unlocking his inherent strengths and weaknesses.

To accomplish this, Sennin used methods as exoteric as scientific observation, to the esoteric, for example, *Junishi-no-jutsu* (Chinese astrology).

Sennin also used techniques like hypnosis (Yugen-shin) on both friend and enemy alike.

Hypnotism was used to help prepare young agents to overcome their fears and allowed them to carry valuable information—information that because of hypnosis they were not even aware they were carrying.

Hypnotism was also used in a variety of ways against enemies. More on this in the Ninth Hall. (For a complete training course in Ninja Sennin mind-manipulation, see Lung and Prowant, 2001.)

The One-Eyed Snake

One of the Sennins' most successful mind ploys was to use a combination of physical and mental means to fake the dreaded "Death's Touch" (Ch. Dim Mak).

We will never know for certain which of the many Shinobi Ninja clans actually possessed the secret of Dim Mak. We do know for certain Sennin were masters of various aspects of traditional Chinese medicine, including herbs . . . the flip side of which were poisons, and accupuncture—the "dark side" of which is the Dim Mak (Omar, 1989).

We do know that, when unable to acquire true Death Touch, Ninja did the next best thing . . . they simply faked it!

Techniques designed to mimic Dim Mak, that is, to kill without leaving a trace, are known as "The One-Eyed Snake"—as in a "one-eye" viper still has two fangs! These included various poisons, asphyxiation, specially designed skewers that allowed Ninja to cut a person's throat from the inside (!) and "icepicks" targeting the brain through the ear or nose—leaving no marks.

The fact that autopsies were unheard of in the East in medieval times made these One-Eyed Snake ploys all the more successful.

Other "One-Eyed Snake" ploys involved saturating a victim's robe with timed toxins. This particular ploy had the added benefit of allowing a Ninja agent posing as an astrologer or priest to read the hapless victim's fortune and (surprise!) correctly "predict" their demise—to the shock and awe of those around him.

More on this in the Ninth Hall: Mysticism.

PROGRESS NOTE: *"CHING AND CH'I"*

Having ventured this deep into the Shinobi realm, the observant student would by now have noticed that whereas the first five of the nine halls are "combat" specific, the remaining four—"higher"—halls are referred to as "arts." Yet, this in no way indicates that the skills to be mastered in these four higher halls are in any way less combat applicable . . . *quite the opposite!*

The tiger is faster than the man, his claws more deadly, but does that make the tiger more cunning, smarter than the man? No.

The tiger's way is a direct approach, while not lacking in stealth, surely lacking in guile.

The way of men, on the other hand, uses both direct and indirect methods to accomplish goals . . . or *should.*

Before combat comes calculation . . . or *should.*

While there is arguably a certain amount of satisfaction in brutally beating down an enemy, Sun Tzu maintains that defeating an enemy *sans* fighting is the consumate skill.

Barring this, bedazzling and blinding a foe into defeat surely takes more skill than bludgeoning him, right?

Sun Tzu thus taught two types of approach: *ching* and *ch'i*, direct force and indirect force. In open combat, ching-ch'i translates into the use of traditional armed forces versus the use of "special forces" (Green Berets, SEALs, etc.).

Likewise, within the nine halls think of the first five training halls as *ching,* direct methods for combatting and overcoming foes, whereas the remaining four halls are more *chi,* teaching us to deal with problems with more subtlety, more calculation—but no less effectively.

Thus, when we can avoid contact with an enemy altogether by use of an effective disguise, obtaining vital—compromising—information on a foe despite his best efforts to prevent us doing so, before then escaping in a puff of smoke or shimmer of mirror, *that* is the consummate Ninja skill! Why? Because it requires using several aspects of Ninja training in perfect concert with one another.

Even more so, what if we could successfully peer into the mind of a foe, first to discern his intentions beforehand, and then defeat him, not by planting a poisoned dirk in his ribs, but by planting suggestions of doubt and defeat in his superstitious mind—*that too* is the Way of the Ninja!

Perhaps you still scoff.

Being of a brutish frame of mind, you still prefer the feel of your enemy's throat beneath your steel fingers. So be it. Nature needs what Nature breeds. What she no longer needs, she discards without looking back.

In such case, simply view these following four "arts" halls as techniques for getting you one step closer to your enemy's *throat!*

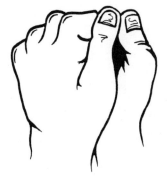

JIN,
"Hidden Hand,"

grants the seeker the attribute of *perception*

and opens the way to entrance into

THE SIXTH HALL:
THE ART OF DISGUISE

INTRODUCTION: *"FRONTI NULLA FIDES"**

The best disguise is not being seen.

We all know Ninja wrote the book on the art of stealth . . . or at least successfully plagiarized enough passages from their predecessors to ultimately make "ninja" synonymous with shadow and stealth.

But for those times when wrapping yourself in the safe embrace of Mother Night is not an option, Ninja must quickly and effectively disguise themselves well enough to (1) *survive!* and (2) *succeed* in their immediate mission.

To accomplish these twin objectives, in this hall students master a variety of tactics and techniques to disguise themselves; stratagems—some complex, most just common sense.

The end determines the means. In other words, what's your goal (end) that requires you to use a disguise (means)? Your ultimate goal will determine the "depth" of your disguise, that is, the degree to which you go to change your appearance, from simply pulling a wig over your head, to radical plastic surgery designed to change your features for good. Is your goal to:

- Disguise yourself to penetrate—and later escape!—an enemy stronghold?
- Instantly distort your "Body Profile" to confuse and lose a "tail" (police, private investigator, or stalker)?
- Or assume a completely new identity and disappear for good?

Whether a famous outlaw, politician, war criminal, or just an average person trying to start over without their spouse, people "disappear" all the time.

---

*"Fronti nulla fides" means "No reliance can be placed on appearance."

For example, there have been claims that the (in)famous outlaw Butch Cassidy didn't die in Bolivia but died peacefully in his sleep in 1934 after having assumed a completely new identity (see *In Search of Butch Cassidy* by Larry Pointer [1988]).

Similarly, Ralph Epperson in his 1985 *The Unseen Hand*, claims Jesse James lived to be 107 years old, and did so by frequently killing and assuming the identity of hapless cowboys who looked like him. Reportedly, one of James's aliases was as U.S. Senator William A Clark, for whom Clark County, Nevada, is named.

Epperson also claims the Ayatollah Khomeini, who seized power in Iran in 1979, was not the same Khomeini exiled by the Shah in 1965. Instead, Soviet agents had infiltrated Khomeini's Shiite movement and replaced the Ayatollah with a Soviet agent.

Martin Bormann, the highest ranking Nazi to escape justice, disappeared after World War II. Since then, he's reportedly been spotted in Argentina and the former Soviet Union (one theory being that Bormann was a Soviet plant within the Nazi Party all along!).

In Japan, professional *yonigeya* specialize in helping people "disappear" from creditors, Yakuza gangsters, and irate spouses *(Los Angeles Times,* January 9, 2003:1a).

Of course, there's more to disguising yourself than just slipping on an eyepatch. In fact, unless you're planning on infiltrating Long John Silver's scurvy crew, sporting an eyepatch pretty much makes you stick out like a sore thumb!

When we hear the word "disguise," we think of actors wearing putty noses (proper name: "prosthetic application"), false wigs and beards, and all manner of outrageous costumes.

Yet just as often, crafting a good disguise is not so much "adding to" (i.e., putting on a Groucho Marx nose, mustache, and glasses) as it is "taking away" (i.e., distorting another's perception of your true form).

For Ninja, such "shapeshifting" is both a *physical* and *mental* discipline.

Physical Discipline

Physically disguising yourself can be as simple as slapping a floppy hat on your head and turning your *reversible* jacket inside out to "lose yourself" in a crowd.

At the opposite extreme, a successful physical disguise can involve physical "props" such as fake facial "appliances" (wigs, beards, glasses, etc.) and accessories ranging from false identification to the type of car you drive or the house you live in.

Other "physical considerations" to round off your disguise include how you walk, your accent—or lack of—hand gestures (cultural, criminal gang signs, etc.), and any other nuance of dress and deportment that allows you to "fit in without sticking out" or, in the event your disguise is "penetrated," your being *carried out . . .* feet first!

Today's student of the Art of Disguise must take every opportunity to study physical disguise traditions, techniques, and, most important, disguise and makeup innovations of both the entertainment industry and the espionage community.

When crafting an appropriate physical disguise, Ninja take into account two considerations: location and timing.

LOCATION

When crafting your disguise, your first consideration is to dress to fit the location, the "stage" on which your disguise will be expected to pass audition.

We pack differently when visiting Florida than when traveling through Alaska. We dress differently when invited to the Oval Office than when visiting "The Hood" . . . or should!

In the same vein, it's not a good idea to disguise yourself as a Catholic priest when infiltrating a rabidly Protestant neighborhood in Belfast.

Medieval Ninja often disguised themselves as Buddhist priests. First, because priests were plentiful and one more orange robe wouldn't draw undue attention. And second, because priests could come and go at will, whereas common folk might be harassed by Samurai.

There is an oft told story of how Samurai Kamiizumi Hidetsuna, the sixteenth-century founder of the *Shinkage-ryu* "New Shade School" of Ninjutsu (so-called since it specialized in pulling "the shade" over a foe's eyes), once disguised himself as a Buddhist priest to first get close to, and then overcome, a deranged man holding a child hostage (Lung and Prowant, 2001:162).

During the infamous "Atlanta Child Murders," one theory proposed was that a white man, disguised as a policeman, deliveryman, meter reader, and so on, might be the one abducting black children. While true that people all too often only see the uniform and not the person in it, common sense argued that such a "disguise" would hardly work in an all-black neighborhood where a white man, no matter his "disguise," would fall under scrutiny the minute he entered the area. FYI: A black man was eventually found to be the killer.

Before deciding on the appropriate degree ("depth") of your disguise, *extensive* study must be made of your "AO," the area of operation your disguise will get you into (and hopefully out of!).

TIMING

Sun Tzu noted that soldiers act differently in the morning and at midday than they do during the evening. In the same vein, people dress differently during the day than they do at night.

In the morning hours, more deliverymen, mail carriers, garbagemen, and so on are out and about. One more man in coveralls or UPS uniform won't stick out.

It's a sorry fact that most of us never consciously register "the little people" around us: valets, janitors and maids, clerks, and all the other "worker bees" and "drones" we interact with on a daily basis—

any one of which could be an enemy in disguise, any one of whom's identity we might be able to assume to accomplish our mission.

Note: The only exception to blending in and not drawing undue attention to yourself when in disguise is when you *want* to be seen, for example, while committing a crime, since you've disguised yourself to look like someone you want to incriminate.

Needless to say, the busier an area, the less time that security guard is going to have to scrutinize your disguise.

Beware: The latest innovation in literally "seeing through" disguises uses *biometrics,* cameras and scanners linked to computers that can shuffle your face through a massive database of known criminals and terrorists. Discovering a match, the computer immediately alerts security personnel.

These computer programs identify you by coordinating and comparing several points on your face (e.g., the distance between eyes).

To "beat" such electronic scrutiny, it will be necessary to *radically* change your appearance (e.g., using cosmetic putty to build up and thus distort the distance between your eyes).

The days of simply glueing on a fake beard to pass muster are quickly coming to an end.

Remember the Ninja saying: There are no new answers, only new questions. Thus, no matter how technologically advanced such detectors become, in the end, some all-too-fallible *human* has to come to check it out.

Thus, even when in disguise and attempting to penetrate a heavily guarded perimeter, have an accomplice cause a disturbance away from your site of ingress, and/or otherwise tie up the attention of anyone who might see through your disguise.

Human frailty has always been the Ninja's best ally.

- ◆ Human beings are more lax around the end than at the beginning of their shift.
- ◆ More lax after eating, after smoking a cigarette, after drinking alcohol, and after sex.

The more relaxed they are, the less likely they are to see through your disguise.

As with all things Ninja, when it comes to crafting an effective disguise, timing is everything.

Mental Discipline

Two "mental" factors help determine how successful a disguise is:

First, the steps taken to disrupt and distort the perception of the enemy, not just by changing your phyisical "body profile" but also by the "vibes" a disguised person puts off, that is, how the disguised agent "carries" himself.

PERCEPTION RECEPTION

As previously pointed out in Lung's *Knights of Darkness* (1998) and Lung and Prowant's *Shadowhand* (2000) and *Black Science* (2001), human perception is all too flawed, all too easily distracted and distorted. This presents a constant danger when it comes to our own safety, forcing us to forever be on the alert to defects and deficiencies in our own perception of the world.

However, this human frailty works to our advantage since our enemy(s) also possess these failings.

For the most part, *people see what they want to see*. As a result of their false prides (i.e., overconfidence) and prejudices, they all too often overlook what's right under their noses, and this includes the people around them.

Ninja count on this.

During the course of his criminal career, accomplished impostor Frank Abagnale, whose autobiography *Catch Me If You Can*

(1986) was turned into the 2002 hit movie, often disguised himself by wearing uniforms, such as an airline pilot's uniform.

Early on, Abagnale realized that *people look at the suit,* rather than the man in the suit.

Big surprise, there's a big difference trying to pass a bad check when you're dressed like a gangbanger than when you're dressed in a three-piece suit.

After abducted teenager Elizabeth Smart remained missing for months, many around Salt Lake City were ready to give her up for dead. Thankfully, the youngster was finally found alive in the spring of 2003. It was soon discovered that for much of the time she was missing, she'd been hidden "in plain sight," dressed in the long robe and veil of a wandering "cult." Disguised this way, the kidnapped girl had once even attended a crowded party where she went unrecognized. Another time, the "cult" was videotaped in a park but the videographer didn't approach the group for fear of "offending" them. This is just what the would-be cult leader/kidnapper counted on.

How we see someone—or ignore them—can spell the difference between our seeing through their disguise—or their seeing through ours.

By researching the prejudices and/or preconceptions of an individual and/or group we will be interacting with while disguised, spells the difference between success and failure.

THE WAY OF "WA"

Ninja call it "disguising your *wa*": Through meditation and mastery of body language, ninja shadowhanders learned to disguise their intention to do others harm. This allowed them to draw close enough to their victims to deliver the coup de grace. Ninja refer to this as masking their *wa*. *Wa* can be translated as "presence," "aura," or "intent" (Lung and Prowant, 2000:69).

When crafting our disguises, care must be taken to coordinate our overall body "attitude" to fit any particular disguise we choose. This goes beyond just adopting appropriate physical mannerisms, to adapting our "vibes" we put off. We do this by consciously releasing body tensions and discarding what poker players call "tells," unconscious ticks and twitches, sweatings and frettings that might tip our hand and give us away.

Novice beekeepers are taught to "visualize" a hexagon to calm their own minds and, supposedly, bring their own mind "into synch" with disturbed bees.

In the same way, Ninja master meditation and "prefight" visualization techniques, both of which can help "balance" and "mask" their *wa* "vibes," making their disguise(s) impenetrable (more on this in the Ninth Hall).

"Disguise" and "Ninja" are almost synonymous.

From perpetuating the myth—and disguise—of being descended from Tengu demons, to medieval Ninja *Jonin* clan masters—out of necessity—keeping two or more identities, even to the point of establishing "rival" Ninja clans, mastering the art of disguise was—is still!—intricate to Ninja survival (see *The Great Clans* in section I).

The world's a cold place. Dress accordingly.

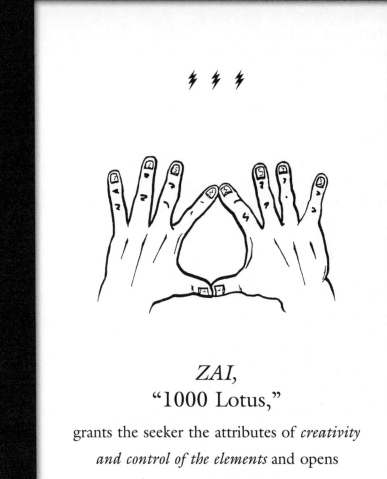

ZAI,
"1000 Lotus,"

grants the seeker the attributes of *creativity and control of the elements* and opens the way to entrance into

THE SEVENTH HALL:
THE ART OF ESPIONAGE

INTRODUCTION: *"THE GREAT GAME"*

When most people hear the word "espionage," they think of James Bond, 007. But for Ninja, "espionage" is as simple as (1) *gathering intelligence* on the "obstacles" standing in your way, human and otherwise, and (2) effectively *neutralizing* those obstacles, either by outmaneuvering them, or else by taking "appropriate steps" to remove them.

Of course, "gathering intelligence" works best when our foe doesn't know we know what he doesn't want us to know.

And "neutralizing" works best when your target never sees it coming, and never knows what hit him—figuratively speaking, of course.

Intelligence Gathering

There are two types of "intelligence": the innate intelligence we're born with, and the kind of intelligence you gather and garner through various means.

INNATE INTELLIGENCE

Not everyone is born with acuteness of perception and quickness of wit. Some of us have to work at it.

The good news is the human mind is infinitely trainable, with an infinite storage capacity for information. And, since most people only use their minds to 10 percent *efficiency,* that means we all have plenty of room for improvement.

Another factor to consider is that *there are different types of intelligence.* Psychology no longer limits the measure of "intelligence" to how well you score on memory and vocabulary. Newer scales of intelligence identify at least seven types of innate intelligence, including spatial ability and artistic and motor adroitness.

GATHERED INTELLIGENCE

What we lack in innate intelligence, we must make up for in gathered intelligence.

There are numerous ways to gather intelligence. And the methodology for doing so is as simple as the rules your mother taught you as a child for crossing the street: stop, look, and listen.

To gather intelligence on anything *and anybody,* all we have to do is hone our innate ability to *observe and listen* to what people are telling us . . . especially when they don't realize they're giving themselves away.

Every time we take a step—literally—we leave behind traces, scraps of our lives, that a wily enemy can exploit to their advantage.

Digital DNA. Every time we use a credit card, we leave behind "traces" that agencies and wily individuals can not only use to track us physically but also allow our credit card company and other "interested" parties to monitor our spending habits. Supposedly, this is done so that in the event a thief goes on a "spending spree" with your card, the company will be alerted to "abnormal spending activity," which is different from your "normal patterns of spending." While this sounds like a good thing, think what such "profiling" tells the credit card company—and whoever they sell the info to!—about you?

Every time you use the ATM, you also leave behind "digital DNA," if only in the form of your picture. Cameras are everywhere nowadays—from store video surveillance, to stoplight cameras, to police cruiser "dash-cams." At any given time of any day, *assume you are on camera and being watched.*

The Poor Man's Internet, the trash can, has always proved an invaluable source of information for police and private investigators.

According to master investigator Kevin McKeown, the author of *Your Secrets Are My Business* (Plume, 2000), trash is still the Internal Revenue Service's most frequently used information-gathering tool: "Do not—ever—underestimate the power of trash! You leave trash behind you more frequently than you leave fingerprints. And trash provides much more information" (McKeown, 2000:30).

The Internet has the potential to link us to every other person on the planet, unfortunately giving every other person on the planet access to information about us. Any computer linked to the Internet can be hacked. Your only safe bet, *keep two computers,* one for personal business not linked to the net: "No matter how many different passwords, levels of document encryption, or redundant security features are built into a computer system, that system's only as secure as the people watching over it choose to be" (McKeown, 2000:146).

Telecommunications. Every time you use a cell phone, you're sharing your secrets with the world. "Private" cell phone conversations are anything but. Cell phone conversations can be easily intercepted using easy-to-acquire, easy-to-construct devices. FYI: All cell phones are now manufactured with a "911" tracker chip that allows law enforcement personnel—and other "knowledgeable" agencies and individuals—to track you via your cell phone, *even when it's not in use.*

Echelon is the National Security Agency's (NSA) global network of fixed listening posts, sattelites, and God knows what else, all allowing the NSA to monitor every electronic communications anywhere in the world. Monitored 24–7 by the latest hi-tech computers programmed to search for "key words," mention "Osama bin Laden" while phoning your Aunt Matilda and someone at the NSA has just opened a file on you.

Ninja Rule: Assume someone is listening. Assume someone is watching. At all times.

Using Spies and Agents

One reason Sun Tzu's *Ping Fa* has stood the test of time is because Sun Tzu was one of the first strategists to place the art of espionage, particularly intelligence gathering, before brute force: "Enlightened princes and wise generals conquer their enemies because, unlike ordinary men, they rely on prior intelligence. This prior intelligence cannot be had by petitioning spirits and Gods, nor by comparing the present with the past, nor even from statistics. Such knowledge can only be obtained from strategically-placed agents" (Sun Tzu XIII:3–4).

In general, gathered intelligence comes to us in two forms: *fixed* and *fluctuating*.

Fixed intelligence includes *physical information* that can be copied, bought, stolen, or bullied, often from a disgruntled employee and/or mercenary worker in just the right spot to slip you the vital information you require.

Often, such intelligence comes from "the little people" (valets, maids, clerks, and co-workers) who daily interact with your target and/or work in an establishment where the desired "intel" is stored. Such "agents" will give up information for a variety of reasons; some simply because they like to gossip or because they have a grudge against the particular person, while others will provide you with information in response to a bribe, blackmail, or bullying.

Fluctuating intelligence assets, on the other hand, are the actual *people* who hold the information you need.

The "fluctuating" part comes from the fact that—big surprise!— the minds of men are forever dancing around, their attention spans short, their particular purposes and motivations fluctuating from day to day . . . okay, *minute to minute!*

As already mentioned, such people can be "approached" through a variety of means. Thus, when deciding on how best to approach these individuals, Ninja employ *Gojo-Goyoku,* "The Five Weaknesses" all humans share.

At any given time, one of these "weaknesses" dominates. Use the acronym FLAGS, as in "warning flags": Fear *(kyosha),* Lust *(kisha),* Anger *(dosha),* Greed *(rakusha),* and Sympathy *(aisha).**

---

*For a detailed course in the practical application of Gojo-Gyoku, see Lung and Prowant, 2001.

Assassination

The medieval Grandmaster of the Persian Hashishins (Assassins), Hasan ibn Sabbah, aka "The Old Man of the Mountain," taught his Islamic "ninja" what has become known as *"Hasan's Rule"*: "All political problems can be solved either through *education . . .* or *assassination"* (Lung, 1997B).

Hasan's reasoning follows that you first try "educating" an enemy, that is, convincing him to become your ally, or at least get the hell out of your way.

Hasan's main way to "educate" his enemies was to have them wake up one morning in their "impenetrable" strongholds only to discover a *poisoned dagger* laying on the pillow next to them. This "visual aid" was usually enough to "educate" even the most stubborn of foes. Other times, bribery paid for the person's "education."

However, every now and then, you run into people . . . "obstacles" who refuse to be "educated." In such instances, according to Hasan, you simply kill them . . . and then you kill whoever takes their place . . . and you keep killing their replacements *until* you get a replacement who *is* willing to "listen to reason," that is, who is willing to be "educated."

Since numbers seldom lie, half a world away, Japanese Ninja had done the same math and come to a similar equation for "educating" their enemies.

The modus operandi of Shinobi *Jonin* was to first seek alliances where able. Should these overtures be rebuffed, warnings were then sent out—the old "dagger on the pillow" type of warning.

When these attempts at "education" failed, Shinobi were forced to resort to assassination.

As cold as this might initially sound, as much as the thought of spending a few cents for a single bullet targeting a merciless dictator—as opposed to millions on a protracted war, might offend our Western sensibilities, consider the argument that a *headless* serpent can't bite anyone. Modern translation: if Hitler had been assassinated in 1933 then World War II might not have happened.

The death of one versus a hundred, a thousand . . . millions?

Ninja understood this equation and, as a result, became the undisputed *masters* of murder—both political and professional—sure, silent, swift, and from the shadows murder.

"There is no place where espionage cannot be used to your advantage. Study well this delicate matter!"
—Sun Tzu XIII:14

RETSU,
"Wisdom Fist,"

grants the seeker the attribute of *will power*

and opens the way to entrance into

THE EIGHTH HALL:
THE ART OF ESCAPE AND EVASION

INTRODUCTION: *"E & E"*

The end is important in all things.

A man can live a righteous life, but if he shames himself in the last minute of life, that will be his only epitaph; all his former fine deeds forgotten.

On the other hand, an otherwise unremarkable fellow can live a mundane, perhaps even reprehensible existence. Still, should the final stroke of his sword serve the cause of justice, or should he commit his last breath to the aid of another, that will be his lasting legacy.

In golf and other sports, it's all about your "follow-through." Likewise in martial arts, the Master teaches that "The most important part of kicking is the landing."

The end is important in all things.

Likewise, it's often easier to get into an enemy stronghold than it is to get out.

All too often, where the utmost care is taken to penetrate—*ingress*—an enemy stronghold, all too little thought is given to *egress*—escape—from danger after the successful conclusion of a mission, which includes evading pursuers.

When a Shinobi Ninja squad was assigned a mission, various members—all experts in their individual craft—were assigned special duties to carry out.

For example, one Ninja's job was to get the team "over the wall," into the enemy stronghold, where a second Ninja was assigned to (1) "take out" any sentries in the way and (2) "watch the back" of additional team members carrying out intelligence gathering and/or assassination assignments.

These Ninja teams always included an "E & E" expert, a Ninja responsible for getting the team safely to the site and then making sure every one in the team made it back home alive.

This Ninja's job entailed not only finding the surest, safest, and most surreptitious route to and from the "area of operation" (AO) site but also the setting up of alternate routes of escape and evasion, including the rigging of traps, trip wires, and other distractions designed to dissuade pursuers.

When a Ninja infiltrator operates alone, he (or she) always plans his escape route ahead of time. This includes alternative routes of escape, all of which should be booby-trapped *during ingress* in the event the Ninja is forced to make a hasty retreat.

The lone Ninja often prepares "bolt-holes" in case hiding is required. Extra weapons and foodstuffs, disguises, and any number of "support equipment" will also be hidden beforehand on or near the AO.

Skills needed to master this Eighth Hall include:

- Mastery of both day and night movement. (Review: the Fifth Hall: Specialized Combat Training)
- Intimate knowledge of the AO: Ingress and egress routes, including alterate routes; coordinating your activity to fit normal activity levels of the AO; appropriate dress and/or cultural norms to be observed (Review: the Sixth Hall: The Art of Disguise)
- Potential bolt-holes (i.e., "safe houses" and hiding places). Each of your bolt-holes, whether a penthouse or an outhouse, should include an emergency first aid kit. Cache of weapons, additional ammunition, and/or foodstuffs should also be hidden along your route of egress. Note: Whenever possible, *booby-trap* your emergency cache (and/or the approach to it) to "punish" accidental discovery by enemy sweeps.
- Vehicles to be used, including alternative transportation in case of an emergency. This should include secondary "pickup" sites (i.e., alternative landing zones)
- Mastery of "Ambush Theory" (i.e., setting up booby traps, explosives, etc.), designed to block pursuit.*

---

*For a complete course on shadow and stealth, ingress and egress, see Lung, 1998.

The nature of a Ninja's existence means that each time he (or she) looks in the mirror, he sees Death looking over his shoulder.

It matters not if that "ninja" is a medieval Shinobi stalking the local *Daimyo,* or a modern-day Special Forces operative "painting" Saddam Hussein's cigar with a laser tracker, helping guide in that "bunker buster."

Ninja dine daily with Death.

For such dark souls, Death is a bosom companion and, in many ways, their only constant, since it is only in comparison to the bitter taste of Death that the true sweetness of Life can fully be appreciated.

That Death will come, we know. That Death will come when we take *this* step . . . or the next . . . or the next, that is by no means certain. That is decided by our dedication to training, our adroitness at avoiding Death's grasping digits.

And while Death must be accepted as the consequence of a slip here, a stumble there, punishment for that second of inattention to that smallest of detail . . . or perhaps just the Universe having gotten up on the wrong side of the celestial bed, that doesn't mean we shouldn't give the Old Gray Mower a run for his money!

The noble sacrifice of one man for his fellow is . . . well, *noble.* But so much less so if that sacrifice—his death in doing so—was not necessary.

Fanatical "martyrs" lick their already blood-stained lips in anticipation of dying for their cause.

Ninja are more than happy to help their enemy die for *his* cause.

Ninjutsu is defined as "The Art of Stealth," but it could just as easily be defined "The Art of Success," of succeeding where others fail. Why? Because Ninja *try* where others fear to try—where failure means capture and torture and death . . . *or else their escaping* to fight another day!

The Ninja's job is to succeed. To succeed, and then to *escape* to succeed again, and again.

Thus, twice as much attention must be put into our "getting out" as our "getting in."

More than any other, this Eighth Hall is the hall where all your other halls' training converges.

It is here that the techniques of stealth and *Taisavaki* "Shadow-hand" techniques you learned in the Fifth Hall prove their worth, helping you shapeshift into the shadows of the night to avoid capture.

Pursued during the light of day, you fall back on the quick-change techniques of disguise you mastered in the Sixth Hall.

You may also find yourself relying on espionage tactics you were taught in the Seventh Hall; not only putting your innate intelligence to the test but also calling on intelligence you've gathered on your AO—as well as any "helpful" natives in the general area who might be bribed (or bullied) into rendering you emergency assistance.

Trapped, your back literally to the wall, in a pinch techniques gleaned during your study of "assassination" in the Eighth Hall— as well as the combat tactics mastered in the first four halls—will also come in handy!

"When your force is in all ways weaker than your foe, avoid him and elude him. The small army is but booty for the big army."
—Sun Tzu, III:17

ZEN,
"The Great Sun,"

grants the seeker the attribute of *enlightenment*

and opens the way to entrance into

THE NINTH HALL:
THE ART OF MYSTICISM

INTRODUCTION: *"SIX SENSES . . . AND COUNTING!"*

"Things are not what they seem. . . . Nor are they otherwise."
—The Lankavatara Sutra

In the previous eight halls, we concentrated to a great extent on mastery of primarily *physical skills,* from unarmed fighting, to physical disguises, to securing physical evidence on our foes.

Now in this Ninth Hall we turn our attention to directly attacking *the mind* of our enemies, while simultaneously strengthening our own mental capabilities via a myriad of concentration, meditation, and other mental "exercises," all designed to further focus our mind.

Mastery of this Ninth Hall will give us control over both our own mind and the mind of our foe by teaching us the full use of all five of our senses: sight, hearing, scent, taste, and touch.

The Ninja's full use of all five senses—working in concert—often gives foes the impression that the Ninja possesses some "Sixth Sense" of ESP.

Shinobi did nothing to discourage this "superstition" that they possessed mystical powers. Quite the opposite. Ninjutsu developed an entire "sub-art" designed specifically to take advantage of a foe's superstitions—*Kyonin-no-jutsu.* More on this in a minute.

Besides playing on the paralyzing superstitions of their enemies, Ninth Hall students are taught techniques of mind manipulation (e.g., inciting a foe's emotions, planting ideas in his head via subliminal suggestion, and using hypnotism to first disorder and then reorder his world), all designed to give Ninja an edge against foes.

Ninja call this strategy *Kiai-shin-jutsu* ("Shouting into another's mind"). It encompasses all tactics and techniques designed to distort an enemy's view of the world around him—destroying his trust in others and undermining his self-confidence.

This black bag of tricks is divided into techniques for first gaining *mental mastery over self,* before then gaining *mental mastery over foes.*

Mastering Self

> *"Know the enemy and know yourself and in a hundred battles you will never be in peril."*
> —Sun Tzu, III:31

Mastery of their own minds allow Ninja to (1) guard themselves against mental attack from their foes while (2) helping them hone those skills learned in the previous eight halls. Think of this Ninth Hall as putting the razor's edge or keen point onto the "weapons" you acquired in those previous eight halls.

In the same way physical *yoga* leads to practical health, so too the "mental yoga" taught in this Ninth Hall leads to good mental health, leading in turn to a "breakthrough" into what's called "nonlinear thinking," thinking that steps outside the logical—predictable!—reasoning sequence, allowing you to bypass your enemy's calculations, to come up on your enemy's mental "blindside" to take him unawares.

While studying in the Ninth Hall, Ninja are expected to master several "esoteric" skills. But rest assured, these requisite skills are not just some arcane "spookism," rather, the nature of Shinobi existence demanded that each possesses a *practical application.*

Beware having your head so far up in the clouds that you stumble into the gaping abyss opening beneath your feet. In other words, if a skill—physical or mental—doesn't help the Ninja to survive and prosper—while depriving their enemies of same!—what good is it?

Skills taught in this Ninth Hall include, but by no stretch of the imagination are limited to:

MEMORY ENHANCEMENT

Techniques such as mnemonic devices, acronyms, and visualizations (see below) help you to better remember names, faces, facts, and *your cover story* when captured and questioned. Memorizing dates and other background information (false identification facts, etc.) is an important part of any successful disguise.

A keen memory is vital to field operations where remembering the twists and turns of an AO can spell the difference between successful ingress and egress, between life and death.

CONCENTRATION AND MEDITATION

Concentration is the key to accomplishing all things.

In a combat situation, whether one-on-one physical combat or combat in a free-fire zone, any lapse of concentration can be fatal.

Likewise, any lapse in concentration when trying to carry off a successful disguise can be just as fatal.

"Meditation" is merely "concentration" taken to its logical conclusion, allowing the meditator to "center" and calm himself at will. This in turn allows him to "free up" and focus his mind—and body—at will.

Down through the ages, mystics East and West have developed an endless number of concentration/meditation exercises, all designed to calm, concentrate, and control the mind.

Concentration and Meditation Exercise: Seating yourself in a comfortable position, take several slow, deep breaths, gently pushing your inhaled breath further down into your lungs until they are completely filled. In the same way, when exhaling, gently push all breath from your lungs before inhaling.

Breathe in deeply, the way you do when sniffing the sweet smell of a flower.

To facilitate these "flower breaths," mentally count "one" on inhale, "two" on exhale, "three" on inhale, and "four" exhale, before starting again at "one."

Having calmed and "centered" yourself, and ignoring all else, listen for the "furthest away sound." From where you are sitting, this furthest away sound might be someone moving around in the room next to you, or a car passing, honking its horn on the road outside.

Now "fine-tune" your concentration by gently "pushing" your concentration further afield, outward, until you hear that jet passing far overhead, that rumble of a coming storm in the far distance.

Finally, "imagine" your ability to hear expanding ever outward— from the building you're in, out into the city streets and then the countryside . . . further and further outward . . .

This exercise not only improves your physical hearing and mental ability to concentrate but it can also put you in touch with your "neglected" abilities of imagination and visualization—both important tools to be acquired in this Ninth Hall.

VISUALIZATION

We are often called on to see things in our "mind's eye." Honing our ability to visualize, far from being "mysticism," serves several practical uses, from better recalling the floor plan of an installation we intend to penetrate, to the overall layout of the AO in which we'll be operating.

Good visualization skills allow us to glance around the corner into a potentially dangerous area, for example, a room where a gunman might be hiding, to "flash" it and then quickly pull back, while retaining the "afterimage" of that room in our mind's eye.

Visualization exercise: After calming yourself with a few "flower breaths," concentrate on this *yantra* for a few seconds to the exclusion of all else:

91. Yantra Meditation Device

Now close your eyes and try to retain the yantra's lighter "afterimage" in your mind's eye. Concentrate on this afterimage until it completely fades, then open your eyes and repeat the exercise.

With practice, you'll find your ability to retain this simple yantra (as well as increasingly complex images) in your mind's eye for longer and longer periods of time.

SELF-HYPNOSIS

Along with methods of meditation that Ninja used to calm and control their minds, they also learned techniques of self-hypnosis they could use to calm themselves in times of extreme stress, enhance their memories, and control pain (see *Yugen-shin-jutsu*, below).

KUJI-KIRI

All the previous techniques of concentration, meditation, visualization, and even self-hypnosis come together in the practice of *Kuji-Kiri* ("Nine Hands Cutting"), sometimes simply referred to as "hand yoga."

According to Eastern metaphysics, the same force that permeates and animates the universe also flows through the human body. In India, this body energy is called *prana* and *kundalini*. In China it is *chi*. Japanese Ninja call this energy *ki* (key).

Down through the ages, various methods of physical, mental, and metaphysical exercises and rituals have been developed to either stimulate or stifle this natural energy flow in the body.

The infamous *dim mak* ("death touch") is the most well-known method developed for interfering with this flow and killing a foe (see *"Ninja Death Touch:* The Fact and the Fiction" by Ralf Dean Omar, *Blackbelt* magazine, Sept. 1989).

Other, more benign methods, were developed to stimulate this flow, helping to direct needed energy to weaker and/or ailing parts of the body. The best known of these methods for increasing, releasing, and directing this innate energy are Indian *yoga* and Chinese *acupuncture*

Likewise, Shinobi used the *sanmitsu* (aka "The 3 M's"): *mandala* (meditation on complex *yantra)*, *mantra* chanting, and the use of *mudra*—often called "hand yoga" because they are believed to direct the body's energies in the same way as do the full-body yoga *asanas.*

These simple and complex hand positions serve both practical and metaphysical goals.

Some mudra were/are used as Freemason-like recognition signs by which Ninja agents recognize one another, offering them en-

KAI

ZEN

HEI-PYO

SHA

RIN

RETSU

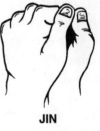

JIN

TOH

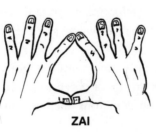

ZAI

92. Kuji-kiri "Nine Hands Cutting"

trance into particular halls of study and, later, testifying to their having mastered that particular hall.

Metaphysically, each mudra practiced is believed to awaken and direct the body's energies toward accomplishing specific tasks.

Traditionally, each Ninja clan and *ryu* ("school") practiced nine particular mudra (similar to nine-degrees of initiation offered by some lower lodges of Western Masonry).

Thus, some mudra are closely guarded secrets of specific clans, while other mudra are universally recognized.

Mastering Others

> *"Ignorant of your enemy and of yourself, in every battle you will find yourself in peril."*
> **—Sun Tzu, III:33**

Ever heard it said "Belief is more important than truth"?

The "truth" may be that there's no way in hell you can overcome a better trained, more heavily armed enemy. Ah! But if that enemy *believes* you can defeat him—that you are more formidable than you actually are—that changes the whole equation.

Your enemy's false belief(s) might cause him to hesitate—to hold some of his "troops" in reserve—at just the right movement . . . *for you.*

Thus the saying "Reputation spills less blood." And Sun Tzu's reminder that "War is the art of deception." And Buddha teaching that "Your best weapon is in your enemy's mind" . . . in fact, it *is* your enemy's mind.

Thus, Ninja went out of their way not just to acquire new physical combat techniques and "technologies," they also did their best to promote an enemy's false beliefs and implant "disinformation" in their foe's mind.

Attacking an enemy's mind is *Saimen-jutsu* ("Storming the mind gate"), since Ninja compared attacking another's mind to breaching an enemy fortress, literally overwhelming their mental defenses, either through direct attack or else entering by stealth and skulduggery.

Saimen-jutsu begins by first determining a foe's overall "mindset" (i.e., how they look at the world), before then discovering—and exploiting!—those inherent weaknesses we all possess.

To accomplish this, the Ninja uses several strategies and skills:

GOJO-GOYOKU ("FIVE WEAKNESSES")

This tactic originated from the ancient Chinese Taoist concept of *wu-hsing*, "Five Elements Theory," the idea that all things in the universe are composed of and controlled by one or more of five basic "elements": Earth, Air, Fire, Water, and Void. Each of the elements either compliment or combat a corresponding element.

Over the centuries, Chinese Taoists catalogued and corresponded these five "elements" to practically *everything* in the world.

Shinobi carried on this tradition by corresponding the *wu-hsing* to five inherent "weaknesses" found in all human beings: Fear, Lust, Anger, Greed, and Sympathy.*

While the potential to express all these "weaknesses" exists in all human beings, at any given time one of these "weaknesses" dominates.

In addition, we develop a "proclivity" to express one of these "weaknesses" more than its fellows. This, in turn, helps determine our overall personality.

By learning to recognize a person's particular *gojo-yoku* "personality," Ninja are able to adroitly craft ploys designed especially to appeal to each person's "weakness."

JOMON-JUTSU

Jomon-jutsu is the skill of using special words and phrases that affect an individual's emotional stability, evocative words that ei-

---

*Use the acronym FLAGS, as in "warning flags," to help you remember these.

MUDRA AND THE THREE STAGES OF MYSTICISM

	MUDRA	ENGLISH NAME	ATTRIBUTE	KEY	HALL	Stages of Mysticism
INTERIOR	RIN	Power Fist	Strength	Strength	Unarmed	PURGATIVE (Detachment)
	PYO	Great Diamond	Focus	Direction of Energy	Wood	
	SHA	Pure-Wind	Healing	Healing	Metal (Sword/Scalpel)	
	KAI	Dragon Hand	Adaptability	Premonition	Flexible	
BALANCE	TOH	Watercourse Hand	Balance	Harmony	Specialized Training	MEDITATIVE (Concentration)
EXTERIOR	JIN	Hidden Hand	Perception	Knowing the Thoughts of Others	Disguise	
	ZAI	1000 Lotus	Control/ Creativity	Control of the Elements	Espionage (Intelligence)	ECSTASY (Enlightenment)
	RETSU	Wisdom Fist	Will	Control of Time and Space	Escape and Evasion	
	ZEN	Great Sun	Enlightenment	Enlightenment	Mysticism	

230

ther inflame him or else lull him into submission (see "Way of the Word-Wizards" in Lung and Prowant, 2001:94).

IN-YO-JUTSU

Tactics designed to "unbalance" an opponent, to sow doubt and distrust in his mind.

In-yo is the Japanese version of the Chinese Taoist concept of *yin-yang* (universal balance). When he is cold, we bribe him with heat. When hungry, we offer him food. When comfortable, we discomfort him.

AMETTORI-JUTSU ("SCARECROW")

This tactic encompasses all tactics and techniques of deceit and deception designed to make an enemy "see" what *isn't* there. This tactic is named for the fact that the form of a scarecrow can easily be mistaken for an actual man.

Employed on a small scale, you drape your coat and hat over a bush at night to make pursuers mistake it for your silhouette.

On a grand scale, during World War II, the Allies "created" an entire phantom army in northern England (replete with fake tanks, planes, personnel, and a strutting General Patton!), convincing the Nazis the Allied invasion force was massing to attack at Calais, France, rather than at the true target, Normandy.

YUGEN-SHIN-JUTSU ("MYSTERIOUS MIND")

This tactic uses hypnosis, subliminal suggestion, and other methods of "Black Science" to influence and control the minds of others.

Many killer cadre down through history, East and West, have successfully used hypnosis to overshadow the minds of others.

Sinan, the Grandmaster of the cult of the Assassins, used hypnosis to both "brainwash" his own followers and influence the minds of the unsuspecting (Lung, 1997).

Even in modern times, unscrupulous individuals have been accused and convicted for using hypnosis. In 1894, a man was hanged for using hypnosis to commit murder (Lung and Prowant, 2001:109).

Ninja *Jonin* used hypnosis against foes. For example, a servant working in an enemy's household can be hypnotized to leave a door or window unlocked.

Ninja leaders also used hypnosis on their own men, giving posthypnotic suggestions designed to strengthen and aid their Ninja operatives. For example, an agent might be given a posthypnotic suggestion that "wipes" his memory clean if captured.

KYONIN-NO-JUTSU

This tactic is the art of uncovering and exploiting a foe's superstitions.

Remember that what people *believe* is more important—and dangerous!—than "the Truth." Why?

Armed with the *objective* "Truth," human beings cannot but act in a logical, thus *predictable* manner.

On the other hand, any psycho can "believe" anything he wants, no matter how fantastic, no matter how little actual evidence he has to support that *subjective* belief.

Thus, encouraging an enemy's superstitious awe and fear was/is just one more way Ninja "get inside the head" of their enemies (see Lung and Prowant (2001) for complete training in the use of *Kyonin-no-jutsu* strategy).

What's that you say? *You* don't have any "superstitions" yourself?

Heh-heh-heh.

Do you still say "Gesundheit" when someone sneezes—a medieval ritual/superstition medieval folk believed would drive away the "devils" who caused colds. Bet you also still believe you can "catch a cold" by walking in the rain. Knock on wood!

CONCLUSION: "The End of the Beginning . . ."

WE'RE TOLD THE "BIG BANG" STARTED THE BALL ROLLING; a cataclysmic explosion the likes of which had never before been seen (or heard).

This begs the question: If a cosmic tree falls in the universal forest, and nobody's evolved enough to hear it, does it make a sound?

The Big Bang also gave us the first instance of the cliché: "If you want to make an omelet, you have to be willing to break a few eggs."

The degree to which a person is able to learn anything is directly proportionate to the amount of sacrifice (and sweat!) he is willing to invest.

Never content yourself with learning any one new thing at a time, nor even learning "something new every day."

Instead, dedicate yourself to mastering "the art of learning." Only then will all things be within your grasp. Only then will you truly begin to learn.

So many "beginnings." A life of "beginnings."

Your deciding to *study to survive* was only the beginning . . .

Your swallowing your fear to step onto the path of privation and pain that winds through the Ninja realm . . . that, too, is only the beginning . . .

Even after you have spent, what? mere *years* to master the rudiments of *Ninjutsu* . . . it is still only a beginning.

And having survived—relatively intact—your sojourn through the Nine Halls on your quest for "mastery" . . .

For true mastery is written, not in ink on some graduation scroll, rather, you will only find it etched in blood on your heart . . . and newly hardened knuckles.

And your true mastery of the Nine Halls will be testified to by the fact you now realize what the neophyte never suspects . . . that your journey through the Ninja realm has only just begun!

Dr. Haha Lung

SOURCES AND SUGGESTED READING

Epperson, Ralph A. *The Unseen Hand*. Publius Press, 1985.

Lung, Haha. *The Ancient Art of Strangulation*. Paladin Press, 1995.

———. *The Ninja Craft*. Alpha Publications, 1997A.

———. *Assassin! Secrets of the Cult of Assassins*. Paladin Press, 1997B.

———. *Knights of Darkness: Secret Fighting Techniques of the World's Deadliest Night-Fighters*. Paladin Press, 1998.

———. *Cao Dai Kung-Fu: Lost Fighting Arts of Vietnam*. Loompanics Unlimited, 2002.

———. *Lost Lo-Han: Shaolin from the Shadows*. Forthcoming.

———, and Prowant, Christopher B. *Shadowhand: The History and Secrets of Ninja Taisavaki*. Paladin Press, 2000.

———. *Black Science: Ancient and Modern Techniques of Ninja Mind Manipulation*. Paladin Press, 2001.

———. *Theatre of Hell: Dr. Lung's Complete Guide to Torture*. Loompanics Unlimited, 2003.

Musashi, Myamoto. *A Book of Five Rings*. 1643. Miscellaneous modern translations in print.

Omar, Ralf Dean. *"Ninja Death Touch: The Fact and the Fiction."* *Blackbelt* magazine, September, 1989.

———. *Death on Your Doorstep: 101 Weapons in the Home*. Alpha Publications, 1993.

———. *Prison Killing Techniques: Blade, Bludgeon, and Bomb*. Loompanics Unlimited, 2001.

Prowant, Christopher B., and Skinner, Dirk. *X-treme Boxing: Secrets of the Savage Street Boxer*. Forthcoming.

Skinner, Dirk. *Street Ninja: Ancient Secrets for Surviving Today's Mean Streets.* Barricade Books. 1995

Sun Tzu. *The Art of War.* 500 BCE. Miscellaneous modern translations in print.